Daily Skill Builders:
Pre-Algebra

By
WENDI SILVANO

COPYRIGHT © 2008 Mark Twain Media, Inc.

ISBN 978-1-58037-445-3

Printing No. CD-404086

Mark Twain Media, Inc., Publishers
Distributed by Carson-Dellosa Publishing Company, Inc.

Table of Contents

Table of Contents (cont.)

Introduction to the Teacher

Both the No Child Left Behind Act and standardized testing require students to meet certain proficiency standards. These Daily Skill Builders are designed to provide students with the opportunity to review or gain extra practice with the skills they are learning in their regular curriculum. They were written with the NCTM National Standards in mind. A matrix correlating the activities with the standards they address is included on pages 1–2.

Suggestions for Use: Each activity page is divided into two reproducible sections that can be cut apart and used separately. Activities could be used in class as a warm-up, a review of a topic covered earlier in the year, as extra practice on a topic currently being studied, in a learning center for review or extra practice, or as a homework assignment.

Organization: Activities are arranged by topic and skill level and are progressively more difficult within each topic area. Activities are designed to cover most areas that are addressed in an average pre-algebra curriculum. The Table of Contents indentifies the skills that each activity covers. Since standardized testing is an important component of education, review activities provide practice in standardized test-taking formats. This helps students become familiar and comfortable with the format and provides test-taking practice.

Topics Covered: Topics covered in the *Daily Skill Builders: Pre-Algebra* book include:

- Fractions and Mixed Numbers
- Decimals
- Integers and Variable Expressions
- Equations and Inequalities
- Graphing in the Coordinate Plane
- Ratios, Proportions, and Percents
- Rational Numbers and Irrational Numbers
- Polynomials
- Probability and Odds

NCTM Standards Matrix for Grades 5–8

NUMBERS AND OPERATIONS STANDARDS	ACTIVITIES
Recognize and generate equivalent forms of commonly used fractions, decimals, and percents	6, 7, 8, 9, 25, 26, 115
Explore numbers less than 0 by extending the number line and through familiar applications	35, 36, 37, 38, 39, 40, 41
Describe classes of numbers according to characteristics, such as the nature of their factors	1, 2, 3, 4, 5
Work flexibly with fractions, decimals, and percents to solve problems	10, 11, 12, 13, 22, 104, 105, 106, 107, 108, 109, 110, 111, 112, 113, 114
Develop meaning for percents greater than 100 and less than 1	104, 105, 106, 107, 108
Understand and use ratios and proportions to represent quantitative relationships	99, 100, 101, 102, 103
Develop an understanding of large numbers and recognize and appropriately use exponential, scientific, and calculator notation	27, 28, 45, 46, 47, 141, 142
Use factors, multiples, prime factorization, and prime numbers to solve problems	1, 2, 3, 4, 5
Develop meaning for integers and represent and compare quantities with them	35, 36, 37, 115
Understand the meaning and effects of arithmetic operations with fractions, decimals, and integers	14, 15, 16, 17, 18, 19, 20, 21, 22, 23, 24, 29, 31, 32, 33, 34, 38, 39, 40, 41, 116, 117, 118, 119, 120, 121, 122, 156
Use the associative and commutative properties of addition and multiplication and the distributive property of multiplication over addition to simplify computations with integers, fractions, and decimals	42, 48, 50, 51, 52, 53, 54
Understand and use the inverse relationships of addition and subtraction, multiplication and division, and squaring and finding square roots to simplify computations and solve problems	123, 124, 125, 126, 127, 128, 129, 130, 131, 132

NCTM Standards Matrix for Grades 5–8

ALGEBRA STANDARDS	ACTIVITIES
Represent, analyze and generalize a variety of patterns with tables, graphs, words, and when possible, symbolic rules	153, 154, 155, 156
Represent the idea of a variable as an unknown quantity using a letter or a symbol and develop an initial conceptual understanding of different uses of variables	43, 44, 49, 55, 56, 132, 133, 134
Express mathematical relationships using equations	49, 57, 58, 59, 61, 62, 63, 65, 66, 69, 70, 71, 72, 73, 74, 75, 76, 77, 78, 81, 120, 121, 122, 132, 137, 138, 140, 143, 144, 145, 146, 151, 152
Investigate how a change in one variable relates to a change in a second variable	57, 58, 59, 61, 62, 63, 65, 66, 69, 70, 71, 72, 76, 77, 78, 81
Identify functions as linear or nonlinear and contrast their properties from tables, graphs, or equations	82, 83, 84, 85, 86, 87, 88, 89, 90, 91, 92, 93, 94, 95, 96, 97, 98
Explore relationships between symbolic expressions and graphs of lines, paying particular attention to the meaning of intercept and slope	73, 74, 75, 76, 77, 79, 80, 82, 83, 84, 85, 86, 87, 88, 89, 90, 91, 92, 93, 94, 95, 96, 97, 98
Use symbolic algebra to represent situations and to solve problems, especially those that involve linear relationships	60, 64, 66, 68, 71, 72, 75, 76, 77, 132, 133, 134, 135, 136, 137, 138, 139, 143, 144, 145, 146, 147, 148, 149, 150
DATA ANALYSIS AND PROBABILITY STANDARDS	**ACTIVITIES**
Predict the probability of outcomes of simple experiments and test the predictions	157, 158, 159, 160, 161, 162

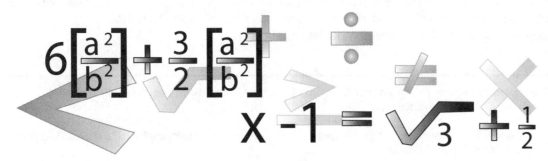

Fractions & Mixed Numbers

ACTIVITY 1 Factors

Name: _____

Date: _____

If a number divides evenly into another number,
then it is a **factor** of that number.

> **Example:** The numbers 1, 2, 3, 4, 6, and 12 will all go into 12 evenly,
> so they are factors of 12.

Answer "yes" or "no" to the following.

1. Is 6 a factor of 30? _____
2. Is 4 a factor of 25? _____
3. Is 5 a factor of 28? _____
4. Is 2 a factor of 18? _____
5. Is 3 a factor of 19? _____
6. Is 11 a factor of 11? _____

Circle the numbers that are factors of the first number.

7. 8: 2 4 5 6 9
8. 20: 2 5 6 10 15
9. 17: 1 2 3 5 17
10. 40: 2 5 7 8 10
11. 32: 2 4 7 8 12
12. 48: 5 6 8 9 11
13. 25: 2 5 6 8 25
14. 60: 3 5 8 10 15

- -

ACTIVITY 2 Determining Factors

Name: _____

Date: _____

For each number, find all of the factors.

> **Example:** 20   1, 2, 4, 5, 10, 20

1. 24 _____
2. 30 _____
3. 18 _____
4. 25 _____
5. 36 _____
6. 45 _____
7. 40 _____
8. 29 _____
9. 21 _____
10. 12 _____

Fractions & Mixed Numbers (cont.)

ACTIVITY 3 **Divisibility**

Name: _____

Date: _____

Tests for Divisibility:

A number is divisible by 2 if the last digit is an even number.

A number is divisible by 3 if the digits add up to any multiple of 3 (e.g., 3, 6, 9,…).

A number is divisible by 5 if the last digit is 0 or 5.

A number is divisible by 10 if the last digit is 0.

Circle the numbers in this row that are…

1. divisible by 2:   5   8   10   30   45   29   36   52   75   484

2. divisible by 3:   9   11   16   27   33   50   24   18   423   780

3. divisible by 5:   11   35   70   28   90   85   43   110   52   895

4. divisible by 10: 59   80   60   44   20   12   70   118   220   350

Bonus: Which of these numbers is divisible by 2 and 3?   28   36   63

ACTIVITY 4 **Prime and Composite Numbers**

Name: _____

Date: _____

A number is **prime** if it is a whole number greater than 1 that has only 1 and itself as factors. A number is **composite** if it is a whole number greater than 1 that has at least one other factor besides 1 and itself.

In this grid, circle all the prime numbers and underline all the composite numbers.

1	2	3	4	5	6	7
8	9	10	11	12	13	14
15	16	17	18	19	20	21
22	23	24	25	26	27	28
29	30	31	32	33	34	35
36	37	38	39	40	41	42
43	44	45	46	47	48	49

Fractions & Mixed Numbers (cont.)

ACTIVITY 5 Prime Factorization

Name:_____

Date:_____

Every composite number can be factored into a product of prime numbers. This is called **prime factorization**. To give the prime factorization of a composite number, first list the number as the product of any two numbers. Then, if either or both of those numbers is not prime, factor them. Continue until there are no more factors that are not prime.

> **Example:** Find the prime factorization of 12: 12 = $\underline{2}$ x 6   (2 is prime,
> but 6 is not.)
>
> Factor 6: $\underline{2}$ x $\underline{3}$ (Both are prime.)
>
> Therefore, the prime factorization of 12 is 2 x 2 x 3.

Find the prime factorization for each number.

1. 44   **2.** 32   **3.** 45   **4.** 18   **5.** 50   **6.** 28

ACTIVITY 6 Using Factoring to Find the Greatest Common Factor

Name:_____

Date:_____

The **Greatest Common Factor (GCF)** of two numbers is the largest number that is a factor of both numbers. One way to find the Greatest Common Factor of two numbers is to list all the factors of each number, and then find the factors they have in common and see which is the largest.

> **Example:** Find the GCF of 12 and 18
> Factors of 12: 1, 2, 3, 4, 6, 12   Factors of 18: 1, 2, 3, 6, 9, 18
> Factors in common: 1, 2, 3, 6   6 is the largest, so it is the GCF.

Use the method described to find the greatest common factor of these number pairs.

1. 20 and 36

Factors of 20: _____

Factors of 36: _____

Common factors: _____ GCF: ___

2. 21 and 28

Factors of 21: _____

Factors of 28: _____

Common factors: _____ GCF: ___

3. 16 and 42

Factors of 16: _____

Factors of 42: _____

Common factors: _____ GCF: ___

4. 24 and 48

Factors of 24: _____

Factors of 48: _____

Common factors: _____ GCF: ___

Fractions & Mixed Numbers (cont.)

ACTIVITY 7 **Using Prime Factorization**
to Find the Greatest Common Factor

Name:_____

Date:_____

Another way to find the **Greatest Common Factor** of two numbers is to first find the prime factorization of both numbers, list all the prime factors the numbers have in common, then multiply the common prime numbers together to get the GCF.

Use prime factorization to find the GCF of each of these number pairs.

GCF

1. 12 and 30

Prime factors of 12: _____

Prime factors of 30: _____

Prime factors in common: _____

Multiply common factors: _____

2. 21 and 35

Prime factors of 21: _____

Prime factors of 35: _____

Prime factors in common: _____

Multiply common factors: _____

3. 18 and 24

Prime factors of 18: _____

Prime factors of 24: _____

Prime factors in common: _____

Multiply common factors: _____

4. 15 and 50

Prime factors of 15: _____

Prime factors of 50: _____

Prime factors in common: _____

Multiply common factors: _____

ACTIVITY 8 **Least Common Multiple**

Name:_____

Date:_____

The **Least Common Multiple (LCM)** of two or more numbers is the lowest number that each is a factor of (except 0). To find the Least Common Multiple, begin listing the multiples of both numbers until you find the first one they have in common (the lowest multiple).

LCM

Example: 3 and 5

Multiples of 3: 3, 6, 9, 12, <u>15</u>, 18, 21   Multiples of 5: 5, 10, <u>15</u>, 20, 25

LCM: 15

Find the LCM of these pairs of numbers:

1. 4 and 6

Multiples of 4: _____

Multiples of 6: _____

LCM: _____

2. 2 and 7

Multiples of 2: _____

Multiples of 7: _____

LCM: _____

3. 3 and 8

Multiples of 3: _____

Multiples of 8: _____

LCM: _____

4. 5 and 9

Multiples of 5: _____

Multiples of 9: _____

LCM: _____

Fractions & Mixed Numbers (cont.)

ACTIVITY 9 **Equivalent Fractions**

Name:_____

Date:_____

Complete to get an equivalent fraction.

1. $\dfrac{4}{3} = \dfrac{\square}{6}$

2. $\dfrac{1}{3} = \dfrac{\square}{18}$

3. $\dfrac{3}{4} = \dfrac{\square}{16}$

4. $\dfrac{3}{8} = \dfrac{\square}{24}$

5. $\dfrac{5}{4} = \dfrac{\square}{12}$

6. $\dfrac{4}{5} = \dfrac{\square}{50}$

7. $\dfrac{5}{8} = \dfrac{\square}{16}$

8. $\dfrac{7}{9} = \dfrac{\square}{45}$

9. $\dfrac{1}{8} = \dfrac{\square}{48}$

10. $\dfrac{1}{2} = \dfrac{4}{\square}$

11. $\dfrac{2}{3} = \dfrac{8}{\square}$

12. $\dfrac{3}{4} = \dfrac{6}{\square}$

ACTIVITY 10 **Simplifying Improper Fractions**

Name:_____

Date:_____

Simplify these improper fractions.

1. $\dfrac{6}{5} =$ _____

2. $\dfrac{9}{4} =$ _____

3. $\dfrac{10}{5} =$ _____

IMPROPER

4. $\dfrac{18}{5} =$ _____

5. $\dfrac{27}{3} =$ _____

6. $\dfrac{20}{3} =$ _____

$\dfrac{24}{5}$

7. $\dfrac{17}{3} =$ _____

8. $\dfrac{29}{5} =$ _____

9. $\dfrac{44}{7} =$ _____

PROPER

10. $\dfrac{33}{4} =$ _____

11. $\dfrac{50}{7} =$ _____

12. $\dfrac{17}{2} =$ _____

$6\dfrac{1}{4}$

Fractions & Mixed Numbers (cont.)

ACTIVITY 11 **Writing Whole Numbers as Fractions**

Name:_____

Date:_____

To write a whole number as a fraction, write the number over the denominator 1, and then multiply both the numerator and the denominator by the same number.

Example: Change 2 to fifths. $\frac{2}{1}$ $\frac{2}{1} \times \frac{5}{5} = \frac{10}{5}$

THIRDS

FIFTHS

Change to halves.

1. 4 _____

2. 6 _____

3. 10 _____

Change to the indicated number.

4. 6 to fifths

5. 8 to fourths

6. 3 to ninths

_____

_____

_____

7. 7 to thirds

8. 4 to sixths

9. 2 to tenths

_____

_____

_____

ACTIVITY 12 **Writing Mixed Numbers as Fractions**

Name:_____

Date:_____

To write a mixed number as a fraction, multiply the whole number by the denominator, and add the numerator. This number becomes the numerator and is placed over the original denominator.

Example: Change $2\frac{3}{4}$ to a fraction.

Whole number (2) x denominator (4) = 8 + numerator (3) = 11

Then place 11 over the denominator (4). $\frac{11}{4}$

M
I   N
X   U
E   M
D   B
    E
    R
    S

Change each mixed number to a fraction.

1. $1\frac{1}{2}$ = _____

2. $2\frac{1}{3}$ = _____

3. $3\frac{1}{4}$ = _____

4. $3\frac{2}{5}$ = _____

5. $4\frac{2}{7}$ = _____

6. $2\frac{5}{8}$ = _____

7. $3\frac{3}{7}$ = _____

8. $6\frac{2}{3}$ = _____

9. $5\frac{2}{4}$ = _____

Fractions & Mixed Numbers (cont.)

ACTIVITY 13 Writing Fractions in Lowest Terms

Name:_____

Date:_____

To write a fraction in lowest terms, divide both the numerator and the denominator by their Greatest Common Factor.

Example: $\dfrac{18}{24} = \dfrac{18 \div 6}{24 \div 6} = \dfrac{3}{4}$

Write each fraction in lowest terms.

1. $\dfrac{9}{18}$ = _____

2. $\dfrac{36}{42}$ = _____

3. $\dfrac{12}{24}$ = _____

4. $\dfrac{6}{30}$ = _____

5. $\dfrac{7}{56}$ = _____

6. $\dfrac{18}{63}$ = _____

7. $\dfrac{20}{60}$ = _____

8. $\dfrac{5}{45}$ = _____

9. $\dfrac{16}{40}$ = _____

ACTIVITY 14 Adding Fractions With Like Denominators

Name:_____

Date:_____

To add fractions with like denominators, add the numerators, write the sum over the denominator, and then reduce the fraction to lowest terms if necessary.

Example: $\dfrac{5}{6} + \dfrac{3}{6} = \dfrac{5+3}{6} = \dfrac{8}{6} = 1\dfrac{2}{6} = 1\dfrac{1}{3}$

Add and put in simplest form.

1. $\dfrac{2}{8} + \dfrac{3}{8}$ = _____

2. $\dfrac{4}{5} + \dfrac{1}{5}$ = _____

3. $\dfrac{3}{10} + \dfrac{3}{10}$ = _____

4. $\dfrac{2}{9} + \dfrac{4}{9}$ = _____

5. $\dfrac{6}{12} + \dfrac{7}{12}$ = _____

6. $\dfrac{5}{11} + \dfrac{2}{11}$ = _____

7. $\dfrac{4}{15} + \dfrac{8}{15}$ = _____

8. $\dfrac{13}{20} + \dfrac{7}{20}$ = _____

9. $\dfrac{17}{18} + \dfrac{6}{18}$ = _____

Fractions & Mixed Numbers (cont.)

ACTIVITY 15 Adding Fractions With Unlike Denominators

Name:_____

Date:_____

To add fractions with unlike denominators, find the Least Common Multiple, change to equivalent fractions, and then add.

Example: $\frac{3}{12} + \frac{4}{6}$ = ? 12 and 6 have 12 as the LCM. $\frac{3}{12}$ stays the same.

Change $\frac{4}{6}$ to $\frac{8}{12}$ Add: $\frac{3}{12} + \frac{8}{12} = \frac{11}{12}$

Add and put in simplest form.

1. $\frac{1}{2} + \frac{1}{3} = $ _____

2. $\frac{3}{8} + \frac{1}{4} = $ _____

3. $\frac{2}{5} + \frac{1}{3} = $ _____

4. $\frac{4}{5} + \frac{3}{8} = $ _____

5. $\frac{2}{5} + \frac{2}{6} = $ _____

6. $\frac{1}{8} + \frac{1}{16} = $ _____

7. $\frac{5}{9} + \frac{2}{6} = $ _____

8. $\frac{3}{12} + \frac{2}{4} = $ _____

9. $\frac{3}{4} + \frac{5}{7} = $ _____

ACTIVITY 16 Subtracting Fractions With Like Denominators

Name:_____

Date:_____

To subtract fractions with like denominators, subtract the numerators, put the difference over the denominator, and reduce to lowest terms if necessary.

Example: $\frac{9}{15} - \frac{4}{15} = \frac{5}{15} = \frac{1}{3}$

Subtract and put in simplest form.

1. $\frac{5}{8} - \frac{1}{8} = $ _____

2. $\frac{9}{10} - \frac{4}{10} = $ _____

3. $\frac{12}{20} - \frac{4}{20} = $ _____

4. $\frac{4}{3} - \frac{2}{3} = $ _____

5. $\frac{6}{8} - \frac{1}{8} = $ _____

6. $\frac{8}{24} - \frac{6}{24} = $ _____

7. $\frac{11}{32} - \frac{3}{32} = $ _____

8. $\frac{15}{25} - \frac{4}{25} = $ _____

9. $\frac{16}{28} - \frac{9}{28} = $ _____

Fractions & Mixed Numbers (cont.)

ACTIVITY 17   Subtracting Fractions With Unlike Denominators

Name: _____

Date: _____

To subtract fractions with unlike denominators, find the Least Common Multiple of both denominators, change to equivalent fractions with that denominator, and subtract.

Example: $\frac{8}{12} - \frac{1}{3}$ = ? 12 and 3 have an LCM of 12. $\frac{8}{12}$ stays the same.

Change $\frac{1}{3}$ to $\frac{4}{12}$ Subtract: $\frac{8}{12} - \frac{4}{12} = \frac{4}{12} = \frac{1}{3}$

Subtract and put in simplest form.

1. $\frac{12}{15} - \frac{2}{5}$ = _____

2. $\frac{6}{5} - \frac{1}{10}$ = _____

3. $\frac{9}{16} - \frac{2}{4}$ = _____

4. $\frac{7}{8} - \frac{3}{24}$ = _____

5. $\frac{3}{4} - \frac{1}{3}$ = _____

6. $\frac{5}{6} - \frac{2}{3}$ = _____

7. $\frac{7}{10} - \frac{1}{5}$ = _____

8. $\frac{1}{2} - \frac{1}{3}$ = _____

9. $\frac{2}{3} - \frac{5}{9}$ = _____

ACTIVITY 18   Adding and Subtracting Fractions in Word Problems

Name: _____

Date: _____

Solve.

1. Mara's cookie recipe calls for $\frac{2}{3}$ cup of raisins and $\frac{1}{4}$ cup of nuts. Her nuts and raisins are mixed. How many cups should she put in her recipe? _____

2. Philip brought out $\frac{9}{15}$ of his baseball cards. He gave away $\frac{1}{3}$ of these cards. What fraction of all his cards does he have left? _____

Fractions & Mixed Numbers (cont.)

ACTIVITY 19 **Multiplying Fractions**

Name:_____

Date:_____

To multiply fractions, multiply the numerators to get the numerator of the product, multiply the denominators to get the denominator of the product, and reduce to lowest terms if necessary.

Example: $\frac{2}{3} \times \frac{1}{4} = \frac{2}{12} = \frac{1}{6}$

$\frac{2}{9} \times \frac{5}{8}$

Multiply and put in simplest form.

1. $\frac{3}{2} \times \frac{1}{4} =$ _____

2. $\frac{1}{3} \times \frac{3}{4} =$ _____

3. $\frac{5}{2} \times \frac{2}{5} =$ _____

4. $\frac{5}{8} \times \frac{4}{5} =$ _____

5. $\frac{5}{8} \times \frac{2}{5} =$ _____

6. $\frac{1}{4} \times \frac{1}{5} =$ _____

7. $\frac{5}{12} \times \frac{3}{2} =$ _____

8. $\frac{1}{2} \times \frac{2}{5} =$ _____

9. $\frac{3}{8} \times \frac{3}{8} =$ _____

ACTIVITY 20 **Dividing Fractions**

Name:_____

Date:_____

To divide fractions, multiply the first fraction by the reciprocal of the second fraction. (Reminder: to find the reciprocal of a fraction, flip it upside down.)

Example: $\frac{3}{5} \div \frac{9}{10} = \frac{3}{5} \times \frac{10}{9} = \frac{30}{45} = \frac{2}{3}$

$\frac{3}{8} \quad \frac{5}{7}$

$\frac{1}{9} \quad \frac{2}{16}$

Divide and put in simplest form.

1. $\frac{5}{9} \div \frac{1}{3} =$ _____

2. $\frac{3}{4} \div \frac{2}{3} =$ _____

3. $\frac{4}{5} \div \frac{3}{3} =$ _____

4. $\frac{7}{9} \div \frac{4}{3} =$ _____

5. $\frac{7}{5} \div \frac{7}{5} =$ _____

6. $\frac{2}{3} \div \frac{5}{9} =$ _____

7. $\frac{3}{8} \div \frac{2}{3} =$ _____

8. $\frac{2}{9} \div \frac{1}{3} =$ _____

9. $\frac{2}{7} \div \frac{4}{5} =$ _____

Fractions & Mixed Numbers (cont.)

ACTIVITY 21 Finding a Fraction of a Whole Number

Name:_____

Date:_____

To find a fraction of a number, multiply the number by the fraction and simplify.

Example: What is $\frac{2}{3}$ of 24?   Multiply $\frac{2}{3}$ x 24 = $\frac{2}{3}$ x $\frac{24}{1}$ = $\frac{48}{3}$ = 16

Solve.

1. $\frac{1}{4}$ of 16 = _____

2. $\frac{1}{3}$ of 27 = _____

3. $\frac{1}{5}$ of 45 = _____

4. $\frac{5}{6}$ of 30 = _____

5. $\frac{3}{4}$ of 36 = _____

6. $\frac{2}{5}$ of 10 = _____

7. $\frac{1}{2}$ of 38 = _____

8. $\frac{2}{3}$ of 18 = _____

9. $\frac{7}{8}$ of 32 = _____

- -

ACTIVITY 22 Canceling in Fractions

Name:_____

Date:_____

When multiplying fractions, you may cancel out numbers that are the same or that have common factors before multiplying.

Examples: $\frac{\overset{1}{\cancel{8}}}{\underset{2}{\cancel{4}}}$ x $\frac{\overset{1}{\cancel{2}}}{\underset{1}{\cancel{3}}}$ = $\frac{1}{2}$ $\frac{\overset{1}{\cancel{6}}}{\underset{3}{\cancel{9}}}$ x $\frac{\overset{1}{\cancel{3}}}{\underset{1}{\cancel{6}}}$ = $\frac{1}{3}$

Demonstrate how you could cancel in each of these problems before multiplying to simplify the problem. Show the cancellations and new factors. Then multiply.

1. $\frac{5}{16}$ x $\frac{4}{5}$ = _____

2. $\frac{8}{10}$ x $\frac{5}{4}$ = _____

3. $\frac{3}{6}$ x $\frac{3}{4}$ = _____

4. $\frac{6}{5}$ x $\frac{15}{2}$ = _____

5. $\frac{5}{3}$ x $\frac{3}{5}$ = _____

6. $\frac{6}{5}$ x $\frac{15}{8}$ = _____

Fractions & Mixed Numbers (cont.)

ACTIVITY 23 Review Adding and
Subtracting Fractions/Test Taking

Name:_____

Date:_____

Fill in the bubble by the correct answer for each problem.

1. $\frac{2}{7} + \frac{3}{7}$ (a.) $\frac{4}{7}$ (b.) $\frac{5}{14}$ (c.) $\frac{5}{7}$

2. $\frac{2}{3} + \frac{3}{4}$ (a.) $1\frac{5}{12}$ (b.) $\frac{5}{7}$ (c.) $\frac{6}{12}$

3. $\frac{3}{5} + \frac{2}{4}$ (a.) $1\frac{1}{10}$ (b.) $\frac{5}{9}$ (c.) $\frac{5}{20}$

4. $\frac{7}{9} - \frac{4}{9}$ (a.) $\frac{11}{9}$ (b.) $\frac{1}{3}$ (c.) $\frac{3}{18}$

5. $\frac{4}{5} - \frac{1}{4}$ (a.) $\frac{3}{1}$ (b.) $\frac{11}{20}$ (c.) $\frac{3}{20}$

ACTIVITY 24 Review Multiplying and
Dividing Fractions/Test Taking

Name:_____

Date:_____

Fill in the bubble by the correct answer for each problem.

1. $\frac{2}{3} \times \frac{3}{4}$ (a.) $\frac{1}{2}$ (b.) $\frac{5}{7}$ (c.) $\frac{5}{12}$

2. $\frac{4}{5} \times \frac{1}{5}$ (a.) $\frac{5}{25}$ (b.) $\frac{4}{10}$ (c.) $\frac{4}{25}$

3. $\frac{7}{8} \div \frac{5}{16}$ (a.) $2\frac{4}{5}$ (b.) $1\frac{7}{8}$ (c.) $\frac{2}{16}$

4. $\frac{3}{5} \div \frac{2}{5}$ (a.) $\frac{6}{25}$ (b.) $1\frac{1}{2}$ (c.) $\frac{15}{10}$

5. $\frac{0}{4} \div \frac{5}{6}$ (a.) $\frac{5}{24}$ (b.) 0 (c.) $\frac{5}{10}$

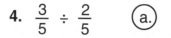

Decimals

ACTIVITY 25 **Rounding Decimals**

Name:_____

Date:_____

Round to the nearest whole number.

1. 42.678

2. 131.009

3. 27.875

_____

_____

_____

Round to the nearest tenth.

4. 35.1876

5. 230.0071

6. 108.876

_____

_____

_____

Round to the nearest hundredth.

7. 609.906

8. 3.4286

9. 26.3111

_____

_____

_____

Round to the nearest thousandth.

10. 1.56789

11. 74.13216

12. 3,256.0985

_____

_____

_____

ACTIVITY 26 **Changing Fractions to Decimals**

Name:_____

Date:_____

To change a fraction to a decimal, divide the numerator by the denominator.

Change each of these fractions to decimals. Round to the hundredths place.

1. $\dfrac{3}{4}$ = _____

2. $\dfrac{1}{3}$ = _____

3. $\dfrac{2}{5}$ = _____

4. $\dfrac{6}{10}$ = _____

5. $\dfrac{4}{8}$ = _____

6. $\dfrac{7}{9}$ = _____

7. $\dfrac{4}{6}$ = _____

8. $\dfrac{1}{12}$ = _____

9. $\dfrac{3}{5}$ = _____

Decimals (cont.)

ACTIVITY 27 **Multiplying and**
Dividing by 10; 100; 1,000; etc.

Name: _____

Date: _____

To multiply by a power of 10, move the decimal to the right as many places as there are 0's in the power of 10. **Example:** 28.6451 x 1,000 ⟶ move 3 places to right ⟶ 28,645.1

To divide by a power of 10, move the decimal to the left as many places as there are 0's in the power of 10. **Example:** 3,567 ÷ 100 ⟶ move 2 places to the left ⟶ 35.67

Multiply or divide.

1. 134.6799 x 100

    _____

2. 33.00085 x 10

    _____

3. 133.6987 x 1,000

    _____

4. 0.45 x 10,000

    _____

5. 28.1919 x 100

    _____

6. 25.69 x 10

    _____

7. 27.007 ÷ 100

    _____

8. 21,345.99 ÷ 1,000

    _____

9. 200,078.13 ÷ 100,000

    _____

10. 29.775 ÷ 100

    _____

11. 456.123 ÷ 10

    _____

12. 0.00007 ÷ 100

    _____

ACTIVITY 28 **Scientific Notation**

Name: _____

Date: _____

To write numbers in scientific notation, move the decimal so that you get a number greater than 1 but less than 10. Then count the number of places you moved the decimal (to the right or left). Multiply the number between 1 and 10 by 10 with an exponent indicating how many places you moved the decimal. Use a positive exponent if you moved the decimal to the left and a negative exponent if you moved it to the right.

Examples: $42,000,000 = 4.2 \times 10^7$ $0.0000975 = 9.75 \times 10^{-5}$

Give the missing exponent.

1. $23,700 = 2.37 \cdot 10^?$ _____

2. $0.00339 = 3.39 \cdot 10^?$ _____

Write each number in scientific notation.

3. 456,000,000 _____

4. 0.000000946 _____

5. The sun is 93,000,000 miles from Earth. _____

6. The water level of the ocean rises about 0.0029 of a foot every day. _____

Decimals (cont.)

ACTIVITY 29 **Adding and Subtracting Decimals**

Name: _____

Date: _____

To add or subtract, line up the numbers at the decimal points, and then add or subtract as normal.

Add or subtract. Write the answers on the lines.

Examples:

$$\begin{array}{r} 1 \\ 49.2 \\ +\ 3.51 \\ \hline 52.71 \end{array} \qquad \begin{array}{r} 2\ 10 \\ \cancel{3}.094 \\ -\ 0.72 \\ \hline 2.374 \end{array}$$

1. 7.3 + 2.9

    _____

2. 13.0 + 9.41

    _____

3. 8.3 + 6.9 + 8.5

    _____

4. 0.08 + 27

    _____

5. 3.376 + 28.6

    _____

6. 1,298 + 2.47

    _____

7. 2.93 – 0.48

    _____

8. 5.74 – 3.8

    _____

9. 75.25 – 18.1

    _____

10. 372.778 – 39.81

    _____

11. 2.078 – 0.1

    _____

12. 432.005 – 12

    _____

ACTIVITY 30 **Multiplying Decimals**

Name: _____

Date: _____

To multiply decimals, multiply the same as for whole numbers. Then count how many total decimal places are in both numbers, and place the decimal in the product with that many places after the decimal.

Example: 3.16 x 1.153

316 x 1153 = 364348

Answer: 3.64348

There are 5 total numbers to the right of decimals in the problem.
Multiply the whole numbers.
Place the decimal so that 5 places are to the right of it.

Multiply.

1. 25.3 x 8.16 = _____

2. 569.1 x 4.2 = _____

3. 7.2 x 0.58 = _____

4. 35.02 x 16 = _____

5. 18.3 x 61.4 = _____

6. 12.8 x 0.155 = _____

7. 12.222 x 1.4 = _____

8. 141.3 x 8 = _____

9. 2.669 x 4.3 = _____

Decimals (cont.)

ACTIVITY 31 Dividing Decimals by Whole Numbers

Name:_____

Date:_____

To divide decimals by whole numbers, divide the same as with whole numbers, but place the decimal point directly above the decimal point in the dividend.

Example: $2\overline{)4.66}$ with quotient 2.33

Divide.

1. $3\overline{)3.75}$

2. $5\overline{)85.60}$

3. $4\overline{)562.464}$

4. $2\overline{)0.6894}$

5. $9\overline{)81.279}$

6. $3\overline{)623.58}$

ACTIVITY 32 Dividing Decimals by Decimals

Name:_____

Date:_____

To divide a decimal by another decimal, first move the decimal point in the divisor to the right until you get a whole number. Then move the decimal point in the dividend the same number of places you moved the decimal point in the divisor. Then divide the same as dividing decimals by whole numbers.

Example: $3.2\overline{)6.464}$ ⟶ move the decimal points 1 place to the right ⟶ $32\overline{)64.64}$ with quotient 2.02

Divide.

1. $0.11\overline{)16.83}$

2. $0.08\overline{)1.48}$

3. $1.2\overline{)3.906}$

4. $2.8\overline{)23.24}$

5. $0.4\overline{)31.2}$

6. $0.02\overline{)0.76}$

Decimals (cont.)

ACTIVITY 33 **Review Decimals/**
Test Taking

Name:_____

Date:_____

Fill in the bubble by the correct answer for each problem.

Select the correct answer showing the decimal rounded to the nearest hundredth.

1. 54.6712   (a.) 54.68   (b.) 54.67   (c.) 55.00

2. 358.13779   (a.) 358.14   (b.) 358.13   (c.) 358.20

Select the correct answer showing each fraction changed to a decimal.

3. $\frac{2}{10}$ (a.) 0.102   (b.) 0.210   (c.) 0.20

4. $\frac{2}{4}$ (a.) 0.5   (b.) 0.6   (c.) 0.25

5. $\frac{3}{4}$ (a.) 0.67   (b.) 0.34   (c.) 0.75

6. $\frac{6}{8}$ (a.) 0.65   (b.) 0.75   (c.) 0.69

FRACTIONS
&
DECIMALS

ACTIVITY 34 **Review +, –, x, ÷**
Decimals/Test Taking

Name:_____

Date:_____

Fill in the bubble by the correct answer for each problem.

Solve.

1. 33.674 + 282.9   (a.) 31.6574   (b.) 316.574   (c.) 3,165.74

2. 987.3 – 22.65   (a.) 964.65   (b.) 9,646.5   (c.) 9.6465

3. (56.4)(32.11)   (a.) 181,100.4   (b.) 181.1004   (c.) 1,811.004

4. 1.98 x 31.3   (a.) 619.74   (b.) 6,197.4   (c.) 61.974

5. 7$\overline{)28.7}$ (a.) 0.41   (b.) 4.1   (c.) 41

6. 0.05$\overline{)3.650}$ (a.) 73   (b.) 7.3   (c.) 0.73

Integers & Variable Expressions

ACTIVITY 35) Integers and Absolute Value

Name:_____

Date:_____

Integers are the set of whole numbers and their opposites. Two numbers are **opposites** if they are the same distance from zero on the number line in opposite directions. **Absolute value** is a number's distance from zero on the number line. You write the "absolute value of 9" like this: $|9|$.

Write "Yes" or "No" to indicate if each of these is an integer.

1. -18 _____

2. 969 _____

3. 24.76 _____

4. $\dfrac{1}{2}$ _____

5. 687.5 _____

6. 99 _____

Write the opposite of each number.

7. 14 _____   8. -3 _____   9. -27 _____   10. 578 _____   11. 32 _____   12. -75 _____

Find the absolute value.

13. $|42|$ _____   14. $|-578|$ _____   15. $|22-4|$ _____

Write an integer to represent each situation.

16. going up 3 floors _____   17. Losing 12 yards _____

18. 7 degrees below zero _____   19. 8 steps forward _____

ACTIVITY 36) Comparing Numbers

Name:_____

Date:_____

Use the number line to help you compare the numbers.
Write <, >, or = to describe how the numbers are compared.

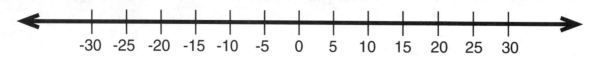

1. 6 _____ 9

2. -17 _____ -14

3. $|25|$ _____ $|-25|$

4. $|-22|$ _____ 0

5. -11 _____ -12

6. 1 _____ -1

7. $|15|$ _____ 15

8. 28.5 _____ 30

9. $|-18|$ _____ $|19|$

10. -6 _____ $|-6|$

11. 0 _____ $|-13|$

12. 4.5 _____ 4.6

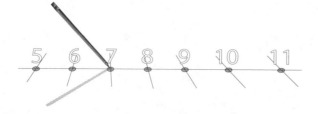

Integers & Variable Expressions (cont.)

ACTIVITY 37 Ordering Numbers

Name:_____

Date:_____

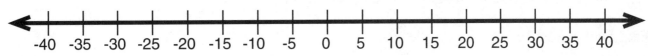

Put the following integers in order from least to greatest. Use the number line above if you need help.

1. 13, -3, 26, -8, 0, -2 _____

2. -4, 6, 7, -11, -1, 2 _____

3. 33, -5, 5, 38, -7, 0 _____

4. -17, 17, -12, 12, -4, 4 _____

5. 0, 6, -9, 11, 16, -20 _____

6. 5, 3, -1, -6, 4, -2 _____

ACTIVITY 38 Adding Integers

Name:_____

Date:_____

Remember, to add integers that have the same sign, just add their absolute values and give the result the same sign as the integers. To add integers that have different signs, subtract their absolute values and give the result in the sign of the larger integer.

Find each sum.

1. 15 + (-12) = _____

2. (-24) + 18 = _____

3. 42 + (-8) = _____

4. 16 + 14 = _____

5. (-15) + 15 = _____

6. (-9) + (-8) = _____

7. (-11) + (-19) = _____

8. 60 + (-10) = _____

9. 27 + 7 = _____

10. 33 + (-8) = _____

11. (-5) + (-25) = _____

12. (-41) + 11 = _____

13. (-3) + 5 = _____

14. $|-39| + |10|$ = _____

15. $|200| + |-97|$ = _____

Bonus: 22 + (-10) + (-16) + 5 = _____

Integers & Variable Expressions (cont.)

ACTIVITY 39 **Subtracting Integers**

Name:_____

Date:_____

Remember, to subtract an integer, just add its opposite.

Find each difference.

1. 11 – 8 = _____

2. 7 – 9 = _____

3. 12 – (-4) = _____

4. (-8) – 4 = _____

5. 36 – 20 = _____

6. 9 – (-3) = _____

7. 38 – 48 = _____

8. 10 – (-16) = _____

9. (-2) – (-2) = _____

10. 20 – (-9) = _____

11. 52 – 12 = _____

12. (-26) – 4 = _____

13. 40 – (-11) = _____

14. (-15) – 5 = _____

15. (-18) – (-40) = _____

Bonus: 25 – (-7) – (-4) = _____

40-17=? ?-9=5 16-11=?

ACTIVITY 40 **Multiplying Integers**

Name:_____

Date:_____

Remember, when you multiply two integers with the same sign, the result will be positive. When you multiply two integers with different signs, the result will be negative.

$$- \cdot - = +$$ $$- \cdot + = -$$
$$+ \cdot + = +$$

Find each product.

1. 6 x 4 = _____

2. 11 x (-4) = _____

3. (-5) x (-8) = _____

4. (-7) x 6 = _____

5. (-8) x (-8) = _____

6. (-14) x 0 = _____

7. 15 x 10 = _____

8. (-3) x 7 = _____

9. (-2) x (-7) = _____

10. 9 x (-8) = _____

11. 12 x 4 = _____

12. (-9) x 6 = _____

13. 10 x (-10) = _____

14. (-4) x (-8) = _____

15. (-12) x 6 = _____

Bonus: 5 x (-4) x (-3) = _____

Integers & Variable Expressions (cont.)

ACTIVITY 41 Dividing Integers

Name:_____

Date:_____

Remember, when you divide two integers with the same sign, the result is positive. When you divide two integers with different signs, the result is negative.

Find each quotient.

1. $18 \div 3 =$ _____

2. $28 \div (-4) =$ _____

3. $(-33) \div 11 =$ _____

4. $24 \div (-3) =$ _____

5. $16 \div 8 =$ _____

6. $(-27) \div 9 =$ _____

7. $(-32) \div (-8) =$ _____

8. $(-20) \div (-5) =$ _____

9. $100 \div (-25) =$ _____

10. $45 \div 15 =$ _____

11. $(-48) \div (-12) =$ _____

12. $72 \div 9 =$ _____

13. $\dfrac{36}{6} =$ _____

14. $\dfrac{-96}{8} =$ _____

15. $\dfrac{(-42)}{(-7)} =$ _____

Bonus: $132 \div (-11) \div 4 =$ _____

ACTIVITY 42 Order of Operations

Name:_____

Date:_____

Remember, when an expression has several components, use this order of operations:

1. Perform operations inside parentheses or brackets.
2. Multiply and divide from left to right.
3. Add and subtract from left to right.

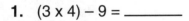

Solve.

1. $(3 \times 4) - 9 =$ _____

2. $6 + (8 \div 4) =$ _____

3. $(-8) + (10 - 4) + 2 =$ _____

4. $6 \div 3 \times 5 =$ _____

5. $(-5) \times (-5) - 8 =$ _____

6. $(3 + 5) + (6 + 7) =$ _____

7. $(-11) - (4 + 4) =$ _____

8. $(16 \div 4) \times (5 + 5) =$ _____

9. $22 - 7(3 + 3) =$ _____

10. $50 \div 5 + 8 =$ _____

11. $(2 \times 7) - 6 =$ _____

12. $14 + 9 - 6 - 4 =$ _____

Bonus: $(16 \times 2) + (8 \div 4) - (17 - 9) =$ _____

Integers & Variable Expressions (cont.)

ACTIVITY 43 **Variable Expressions**

Name: _____

Date: _____

A **variable** is a letter or symbol that stands for a number.
A **variable expression** is a group of numbers, variables, and operations.

Write a variable expression for each phrase (use *n* for the variable)

1. a number plus 7

   _____

2. 8 less than a number

   _____

3. twice a number

   _____

4. the sum of a number and 12

   _____

5. the product of a number and 5

   _____

6. the difference of a number and (-8)

   _____

7. a number increased by twice a number

   _____

8. 3 more than the absolute value of a number

   _____

9. four times a number plus one less than the number _____

ACTIVITY 44 **Evaluating Variable Expressions**

Name: _____

Date: _____

To evaluate a variable expression for given terms, substitute the numbers for the variables.

Example: $3n$ Evaluate the expression for $n = 3$. Substitute 3 for n. $3(3) = 9$

$8 + (10 \times \underline{}) = 38$

$(5 - 2) + \underline{} = 21$

$3^2 \times (\underline{} - 4) = 18$

Evaluate each expression for $n = 5$, $x = 3$, and $y = 2$.

1. $n + 5 = $ _____

2. $x - (-4) = $ _____

3. $3y = $ _____

4. $4x - 4 = $ _____

5. $3y - y = $ _____

6. $3n - x = $ _____

7. $\dfrac{n + x}{y} = $ _____

8. $\dfrac{12 - y}{n} = $ _____

9. $(6n + x - y) = $ _____

10. $x^2 = $ _____

11. $n - 5 + (x + 4) = $ _____

12. $y^3 - 1 = $ _____

Integers & Variable Expressions (cont.)

ACTIVITY 45 Exponents

Name:_____

Date:_____

A repeated factor is called the **base**, and the **exponent** tells how many times the factor is multiplied by itself. The exponent is the small number to the right of the base.

> ***Example:*** 7^4 7 is the base and ^{4} is the exponent. $7^4 = 7 \cdot 7 \cdot 7 \cdot 7 = 2{,}401$
> **Note:** The dot or parentheses will be used to represent multiplication from this point on to avoid confusion with the variable x.

Write each expression using a single exponent.

1. $6 \cdot 6 \cdot 6 =$ _____

2. $4 \cdot 4 \cdot 4 \cdot 4 =$ _____

3. $5 \cdot 5 =$ _____

4. $x \cdot x \cdot x \cdot x \cdot x =$ _____

5. $(\text{-}7)\,(\text{-}7)\,(\text{-}7) =$ _____

6. $(\text{-}b)\,(\text{-}b) =$ _____

Write each expression as a product of repeated factors.

7. $11^2 =$ _____

8. $7^3 =$ _____

9. $\text{-}4^4 =$ _____

Evaluate.

10. $2^3 =$ _____

11. $(\text{-}5)^4 =$ _____

12. x^2 if $x = 9$ _____

- -

ACTIVITY 46 Multiplying and Dividing Exponents

Name:_____

Date:_____

To **multiply** numbers or variables with the same base, add the exponents.
To **divide** numbers or variables with the same base, subtract the exponents.

> ***Examples:*** $2^2 \cdot 2^4 = 2^{2+4} = 2^6$ $5^9 \div 5^4 = 5^{9-4} = 5^5$

Write each expression using a single exponent.

1. $7^3 \cdot 7^5 =$ _____

2. $9^8 \div 9^4 =$ _____

3. $r^6 \cdot r^3 =$ _____

4. $m^7 \div m^2 =$ _____

Use a calculator to evaluate.

5. $3^4 \cdot 3^3 =$ _____

6. $6^8 \div 6^3 =$ _____

7. $2^5 \cdot 2^4 =$ _____

8. $\dfrac{7^7}{7^4} =$ _____

25

Integers & Variable Expressions (cont.)

ACTIVITY 47 **Negative Exponents**

Name:_____

Date:_____

A **negative exponent** is made positive by moving the exponent from the numerator to the denominator.

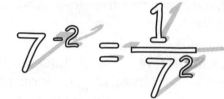

Examples: $6^{-4} = \dfrac{1}{6^4}$ $2b^{-3} = \dfrac{2}{b^3}$

Write each expression using positive exponents.

1. 8^{-2} _____   **2.** n^{-15} _____   **3.** 5^{-5} _____   **4.** xy^{-3} _____

Write each fraction as an expression with negative exponents.

5. $\dfrac{1}{4^6}$ **6.** $\dfrac{1}{11^2}$ **7.** $\dfrac{x}{y^5}$ **8.** $\dfrac{m}{n^4}$

_____   _____   _____   _____

ACTIVITY 48 **Order of Operations**

Name:_____

Date:_____

Remember the order of operations:
1. Perform anything in parentheses or brackets first.
2. Evaluate the exponents.
3. Multiply and divide from left to right.
4. Add and subtract from left to right.

Evaluate each expression.

1. $3^2 + (3 \cdot 4) - 6 =$ _____

2. $7 + 8 - 3^2 =$ _____

3. $[18 - 3] \cdot 3 - 5 =$ _____

4. $(2 + 8) \div 2 \cdot 4^2 =$ _____

Evaluate each expression for the given number.

5. $a^2 + (9 - 4)$; $a = 2$ _____

6. $(x - 3)^3 + 16 - (5 + x) \cdot 2$; $x = 4$ _____

7. $b^2 + [4b - 2] \div 2$; $b = 4$ _____

8. $3^m + (2 + 1)^{m-1}$; $m = 2$ _____

Integers & Variable Expressions (cont.)

ACTIVITY 49 **Writing Variable**

Expressions for Real World Problems

Name: _____

Date: _____

1. Marco earns $7 per hour. He works a different number of hours each week. Write a variable expression to express how much he earns each week. Use the variable *h* for hours. _____

2. Malika sells lemonade for $0.50 a cup. Write a variable expression to show how much she earns depending on how many cups she sells. Use the variable *c* for cups. _____

3. Elio is 2 years older than his brother. Write a variable expression to show how old Elio is when his brother is at various ages. Use the variable *b* for the age of the brother. _____

4. There are 200 seats in a theater. Write a variable expression to show how many seats are empty at any given performance. Use the variable *s* for seats that are full. _____

- -

ACTIVITY 50 **Properties of Numbers**

Name: _____

Date: _____

Match the examples with which property of numbers is represented.

_____ 1. Commutative Property

a. $5 + 0 = 5$ $n + 0 = n$

_____ 2. Associative Property

b. $4 + 5 = 5 + 4$ $x + y = y + x$

_____ 3. Distributive Property

c. $3(2 + 3) = (3 \cdot 2) + (3 \cdot 3)$

$a(b + c) = (a \cdot b) + (a \cdot c)$

_____ 4. Identity Property

d. $(2 + 3) + 6 = 2 + (3 + 6)$

$(x + y) + z = x + (y + z)$

NUMBER PROPERTIES

Integers & Variable Expressions (cont.)

ACTIVITY 51 **Commutative Property**

Name:_____

Date:_____

Reminder: The **commutative property** states that when you change the order of addends or factors, you do not change the result. Addition and multiplication have this property.

Examples: $4 + 7 = 7 + 4$ $3 \cdot 8 = 8 \cdot 3$

$x + y = y + x$ $x \cdot y = y \cdot x$

[handwritten: $10 + X = 32$ B·5·13 $Y + X = 17$]

Write each equation in a different way by using the commutative property.

1. $c + 7 = 15$ _____

2. $3 \cdot d = 12$ _____

3. $8 + m = 10$ _____

4. $k \cdot 6 = 30$ _____

5. $x + 11 = 21$ _____

6. $r \cdot 4 = 16$ _____

7. $y + x + z = 28$ _____

8. $7 \cdot s = 42$ _____

9. $2 + 5 + 9 = 16$ _____

10. $p \cdot q = 72$ _____

ACTIVITY 52 **Associative Property**

Name:_____

Date:_____

Reminder: The **associative property** states that changing the groupings of addends or factors does not change the result. Addition and multiplication have this property.

Examples: $(3 + 8) + 4 = 3 + (8 + 4)$ $(4 \cdot 2) \cdot 6 = 4 \cdot (2 \cdot 6)$

$(x + y) + z = x + (y + z)$ $(a \cdot b) \cdot c = a \cdot (b \cdot c)$

Place parentheses in these expressions to make the computation easier. Then compute.

1. $45 + 55 + 38$ _____

2. $43 + 92 + 8$ _____

3. $6 + 4 + 37$ _____

4. $36 + 12 + 8$ _____

5. $31 + 9 + 15 + 5$ _____

6. $4 \cdot 5 \cdot 7$ _____

7. $48 \cdot 2 \cdot 5$ _____

8. $20 \cdot 5 \cdot 39$ _____

9. $10 \cdot 10 \cdot 15 \cdot 10$ _____

10. $-2 \cdot 5 \cdot 96$ _____

Integers & Variable Expressions (cont.)

ACTIVITY 53 **Distributive Property**   Name:_____

Date:_____

Reminder: The **distributive property** states that if x, y, and z are any numbers, then $x(y + z) = xy + xz$ and $x(y - z) = xy - xz$.

Examples: $4(3 + 2) = (4 \cdot 3) + (4 \cdot 2) = 20$ $3(7 - 3) = (3 \cdot 7) - (3 \cdot 3) = 12$

Rewrite each expression using the distributive property. Do not simplify.

1. $5(4 + 5)$ _____

2. $w(4 + 9)$ _____

3. $6(m + n)$ _____

4. $3(4b + 3c)$ _____

Simplify each expression by using the distributive property.

5. $2(v + 3) + 7v$ _____

6. $3(h + 4) + 7h$ _____

7. $5g + 6(2g + 3)$ _____

8. $7s + 4s + 4(2s + 5)$ _____

ACTIVITY 54 **Properties of Zero and One**   Name:_____

Date:_____

Reminder: Properties of zero and one can make computations much simpler.

Identity property of addition: The sum of any number and 0 is that number.
  Examples: $23 + 0 = 23$ $-509 + 0 = -509$ $n + 0 = n$
Identity property of multiplication: The product of any number and 1 is that number.
  Examples: $7 \cdot 1 = 7$ $-96 \cdot 1 = -96$ $n \cdot 1 = n$
Multiplication property of 0: The product of any number and 0 is 0.
  Examples: $2{,}845 \cdot 0 = 0$ $-2 \cdot 0 = 0$ $n \cdot 0 = 0$

Solve each expression mentally.

1. $47 + (16 - 16) =$ _____

2. $(94 - 93) \cdot 72 =$ _____

3. $\dfrac{87}{87} \cdot 65 =$ _____

4. $(72 \cdot 0) \cdot 13 =$ _____

5. $(18 \cdot 0) + 46 =$ _____

6. $\left(\dfrac{3}{3} \cdot \dfrac{4}{4}\right) \cdot 69 =$ _____

7. $(368 - 368) \cdot 455 =$ _____

8. $32 \cdot [7 - (3 + 3)] =$ _____

Equations & Inequalities

ACTIVITY 55 **Combining Like Terms**

Name:_____

Date:_____

Combine like terms to simplify.

1. $2x + 3y + 3x$

_____

2. $t + 4s - 2s$

_____

3. $3m - 6n + 2m + 4n$

_____

4. $2a - 4b + 3a$

_____

5. $7c - 4d + 3c$

_____

6. $2f - 4g + 6g - 3f$

_____

7. $j - h + 3j - 4h$

_____

8. $5w + 3w + 2w + 7v$

_____

9. $3y - y + 4z + 2z$

_____

10. $6a + 2b + 3c - 2c + 3b$

_____

11. $4h + 2i + 3j - 2h - i$

_____

12. $m + n + p - m + 2n$

_____

ACTIVITY 56 **Simplifying Variable Expressions**

Name:_____

Date:_____

Simplify each expression.

1. $4(x + 3)$

_____

2. $8(m - 6)$

_____

3. $3(2b - 1)$

_____

4. $-4n(2 + 2)$

_____

5. $2(x + 4) - x$

_____

6. $5c + 3(c - 2)$

_____

7. $6(2m - 4) - 2$

_____

8. $9(g + h)$

_____

9. $2(d + 4) + c - 1$

_____

10. $-5x - 4y + 2(3y - 1)$

_____

11. $-4 + 3(b - 2)$

_____

12. $5(a + b) - a - b$

_____

Equations & Inequalities (cont.)

ACTIVITY 57 Solving Equations **by Subtracting**

Name:_____

Date:_____

To solve an equation, you use **inverse operations** to isolate the variable on one side. Use subtraction (the inverse operation of addition) to isolate the variable in these equations.

1. $y + 9 = 12$ _____

2. $6 + m = 11$ _____

3. $10 + b = 15$ _____

4. $z + 3 = 7$ _____

5. $n + 6 = 20$ _____

6. $x + 4 = 4$ _____

7. $8 + m = 4$ _____

8. $z + 6 = -2$ _____

9. $w + 7 = 7$ _____

10. $n + 5 = -1$ _____

ACTIVITY 58 Solving Equations **by Adding**

Name:_____

Date:_____

To solve an equation, you use **inverse operations** to isolate the variable on one side. Use addition (the inverse operation of subtraction) to isolate the variable in these equations.

1. $b - 4 = 2$ _____

2. $m - 6 = 5$ _____

3. $n - 11 = 0$ _____

4. $(-6) + y = 4$ _____

5. $a - 8 = 1$ _____

6. $(-4) + v = 0$ _____

7. $(-2) + t = 5$ _____

8. $c - 3 = 2$ _____

9. $m - 17 = 20$ _____

10. $b - \frac{1}{2} = \frac{1}{2}$ _____

Equations & Inequalities (cont.)

ACTIVITY 59 Solving Equations
by Adding or Subtracting

Name:_____

Date:_____

Choose the appropriate inverse operation to solve these equations.

1. $m + 4 = 9$ _____

2. $b - 4 = 11$ _____

3. $8 + n = 4$ _____

4. $3 + v = 6$ _____

5. $s - 9 = 7$ _____

6. $(-4) + g = 2$ _____

7. $y + (-3) = 6$ _____

8. $k - 4 = 4$ _____

9. $20 + z = 23$ _____

10. $h - 15 = 12$ _____

ACTIVITY 60 Problem Solving
With Equations

Name:_____

Date:_____

Write an equation to represent the situation, and then solve by adding or subtracting.

1. Mike earned $28 on Monday. On Wednesday, he earned some more money. He earned $42 total. How much did Mike earn on Wednesday?

   _____

2. Allysa made some cookies. She took 24 to school for a bake sale. She has 30 left. How many cookies did she make?

   _____

3. Tino bought a CD for $15.98. He got $4.02 for change. How much did he give the cashier?

   _____

4. Milo did 58 homework problems right after school. He did the rest in the evening. If he did 80 problems all together, how many did he do in the evening?

   _____

Equations & Inequalities (cont.)

ACTIVITY 61 Solving Equations
by Dividing

Name:_____

Date:_____

To solve an equation, you use **inverse operations** to isolate the variable on one side. Use division (the inverse operation of multiplication) to isolate the variable in these equations.

1. $6m = 48$ _____

2. $4t = 16$ _____

3. $8a = 72$ _____

4. $5x = 55$ _____

5. $7p = 21$ _____

6. $9z = 90$ _____

7. $-4y = 28$ _____

8. $-7g = -42$ _____

9. $9t = 3$ _____

10. $100j = 25$ _____

ACTIVITY 62 Solving Equations
by Multiplying

Name:_____

Date:_____

To solve an equation, you use **inverse operations** to isolate the variable on one side. Use multiplication (the inverse operation of division) to isolate the variable in these equations.

1. $\dfrac{x}{4} = 5$ _____

2. $\dfrac{m}{2} = 8$ _____

3. $\dfrac{g}{5} = 10$ _____

4. $\dfrac{n}{6} = 0$ _____

5. $\dfrac{w}{-3} = -4$ _____

6. $\dfrac{k}{-2} = 6$ _____

7. $\dfrac{h}{15} = 3$ _____

8. $\dfrac{c}{11} = 9$ _____

9. $\dfrac{v}{-6} = -9$ _____

10. $\dfrac{t}{7} = 7$ _____

Equations & Inequalities (cont.)

ACTIVITY 63 Solving Equations by Dividing or Multiplying

Name: _____

Date: _____

Choose the appropriate inverse operation to solve these equations.

1. $\frac{a}{-3} = 5$ _____

2. $6b = 36$ _____

3. $8n = 48$ _____

4. $\frac{w}{7} = 5$ _____

5. $\frac{y}{4} = 9$ _____

6. $3x = 36$ _____

7. $-12u = 60$ _____

8. $\frac{r}{6} = 8$ _____

9. $\frac{d}{-4} = -4$ _____

10. $5g = 45$ _____

- -

ACTIVITY 64 Problem Solving Using Equations

Name: _____

Date: _____

Write an equation to represent the situation, and then solve by dividing or multiplying.

1. Gregorio has to make 84 cookies for scout camp. How many dozen cookies is that?

_____

2. Zola bought 9 candy bars. She spent $4.05. How much did each bar cost?

_____

3. Jahim will buy a video game that costs $54 in 6 weeks. How much must he save each week to have enough money by then?

_____

4. Tila sold 8 pencils at $1.95 each. How much money did she earn?

_____

Equations & Inequalities (cont.)

ACTIVITY 65 **Solving Two-Step Equations** Name:_____

Date:_____

To solve equations, sometimes it is necessary to perform
more than one step. Solve these equations using whatever inverse operations are needed.

1. $6x - 5 = 7$ _____

2. $-5 = 3y - 14$ _____

3. $4m + 4 = 16$ _____

4. $3d - 4 = 8$ _____

5. $-7 = 9 + 2h$ _____

6. $11n - 6 = 60$ _____

7. $32 = 12b - 4$ _____

8. $18 = 2f + 2$ _____

9. $5a + 9 = 29$ _____

10. $3p - 15 = -6$ _____

ACTIVITY 66 **Solving Two-Step Equations** Name:_____

Date:_____

Solve.

1. $\dfrac{t}{4} - 1 = 10$ _____

2. $\dfrac{b}{3} + 8 = 13$ _____

3. $6 - \dfrac{x}{2} = 2$ _____

4. $12 + \dfrac{m}{7} = 15$ _____

5. $-11 + \dfrac{z}{5} = -7$ _____

6. $\dfrac{w}{-3} + 8 = 5$ _____

7. $\dfrac{y}{9} - 4 = 6$ _____

8. $-6 + \dfrac{r}{2} = 3$ _____

9. $14 = \dfrac{u}{4} - (-9)$ _____

10. $\dfrac{p}{-8} - 7 = -11$ _____

Equations & Inequalities (cont.)

ACTIVITY 67 **Problem Solving by Writing and Solving Equations**

Name:_____

Date:_____

Write an equation for each problem and solve.

_____ ·8+12=60

1. If you multiply a number by 8 and add 12, you get 60. What is the number?

_____

2. Three more than 7 times a number is 38. What is the number?

_____

3. The sum of 5 times a number and 10 is 55. What is the number?

_____

4. If you divide a number by 4 and add 7, you get 15. What is the number?

_____

5. Five less than 9 times a number is 31. What is the number?

_____

ACTIVITY 68 **Problem Solving Using Equations/Test Practice**

Name:_____

Date:_____

Fill in the bubble next to the correct equation that would allow you to solve the problem.

1. If you divide a number by 7 and take away 4, you get 4. Which equation would you use?

   a. $7n - 4 = 4$ b. $\dfrac{n}{7} - 4 = 4$ c. $\dfrac{4}{7} - n = 4$

2. Five more than 4 times a number is 33. Which equation would you use?

   a. $4n + 5 = 33$ b. $4n - 5 = 33$ c. $\dfrac{4}{n} + 5 = 33$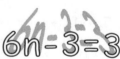

3. Three less than a number divided by 6 is 3. Which equation would you use?

   a. $6n - 3 = 3$ b. $\dfrac{n}{6} - 3 = 3$ c. $\dfrac{6}{n} - 3 = 3$

4. Two more than 7 times a number is 30. Which equation would you use?

   a. $2n + 7 = 30$ b. $7n + 30 = 2$ c. $7n + 2 = 30$

Equations & Inequalities (cont.)

ACTIVITY 69 Simplifying and Solving Equations

Name: _____

Date: _____

First simplify each equation by combining like terms, and then solve.

1. $x + 4x - 3 = 22$ _____

2. $2n + 3n - 7 = 13$ _____

3. $6b + 9 - 2b = 21$ _____

4. $t + 3t = -8$ _____

5. $3s + 10 - 5s = -2$ _____

6. $y - 7 - 6y = -47$ _____

7. $4t + 16 + 2t = 28$ _____

8. $46 - 2r + 3r = 53$ _____

9. $3m + 12 - m = 78$ _____

10. $-3p + 5p + 4 = -6$ _____

ACTIVITY 70 Simplifying and Solving Equations

Name: _____

Date: _____

First simplify each equation, and then solve.

1. $2(n - 4) + 3n = 37$ _____

2. $4z + 3(z + 2) = 34$ _____

3. $-3(2t - 4) + 11 = -7$ _____

4. $7(k - 6) + 8 = -13$ _____

5. $4(r + 3) - 3r = 19$ _____

6. $2c + 2(c - 6) = 72$ _____

7. $9(h - 1) + h = 11$ _____

8. $-2(t - 3) + 8 = 24$ _____

9. $8(g + 2) + 3(g - 2) = 76$ _____

10. $6(j - 7) + 5(2j + 3) = 37$ _____

Equations & Inequalities (cont.)

ACTIVITY 71 **Formulas**

Name: _____

Date: _____

Formulas are written as mathematical sentences, showing the relationship between certain quantities. Below are some common formulas.

distance traveled = rate · time $\qquad d = rt$

perimeter of rectangle = 2 · length plus 2 · width $\quad p = 2l + 2w$

area of a triangle = one half the base · height $\qquad A = \dfrac{1}{2}(b \cdot h)$

Use the formulas to solve these problems.

1. What distance did a car travel that went 70 mph for 6 hours? _____

2. What is the perimeter of a rectangle with a length of 7 cm and a width of 4 cm?
   _____

3. What is the area of a triangle with a base of 10 in. and a height of 8 in.?
   _____

4. How far did a train travel that went 90 mph for 11 hours? _____

5. What is the perimeter of a rectangle with a width of 9 in. and a length of 12 in.?
   _____

6. What is the area of a triangle with a base of 6 cm and a height of 9 cm?
   _____

ACTIVITY 72 **Formulas**

Name: _____

Date: _____

Sometimes, in order to use a formula to solve a problem, you must first rearrange the formula so that the unknown quantity is alone on one side of the equation.

Example: Find the rate at which a car traveled that went 120 miles in 3 hours.

The unknown quantity is rate. Distance = rate x time ($d = rt$). Get r alone by dividing both sides by t. $\dfrac{d}{t} = r$. Then plug in the known information to solve. $\dfrac{120}{3} = r = 40$ mph.

Write the appropriate formula and solve.

1. How long did it take a plane flying 400 mph to travel 2,400 miles? _____

2. How fast did a car travel if it went 300 miles in 5 hours? _____

3. What is the width of a rectangle that has a length of 6 and a perimeter of 18? (Hint: $p = 2l + 2w$) _____

4. What is the length of rectangle that has a width of 7 and a perimeter of 24?
   _____

Equations & Inequalities (cont.)

ACTIVITY 73   Inequalities

Name:_____

Date:_____

Circle the numbers below that are a solution of $x \le -2$.

1. -5   **2.** 3   **3.** 0   **4.** -2   **5.** -1

Write an inequality for each sentence.

6. Joe will need to earn at least $46 to buy his bike. _____

7. The maximum number of passengers that the plane will hold is 200. _____

8. To ride the roller coaster, you must be at least 52 inches tall. _____

9. Each bag must weigh at least 6 pounds. _____

10. There are fewer than a dozen cookies left in the jar. _____

ACTIVITY 74   Graphing Inequalities

Name:_____

Date:_____

Write an inequality for each graph.

1. _____

2. _____

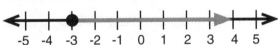

3. _____

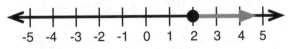

4. _____

5. _____

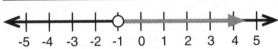

6. _____

7. _____

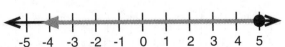

8. _____

Equations & Inequalities (cont.)

ACTIVITY 75 Graphing Inequalities

Name:_____

Date:_____

Graph each of these inequalities.

1. $y < 4$

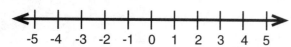

2. $x \leq 2$

3. $t \geq -1$

4. $b > 0$

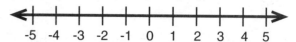

5. $a > -3$

6. $c \geq -5$

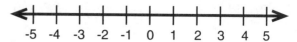

7. $d > 2$

8. $g \leq 5$

ACTIVITY 76 Solving Inequalities by Adding and Subtracting

Name:_____

Date:_____

Solve each inequality by adding or subtracting. Then graph the solution.

1. $x + 2 < 4$ _____

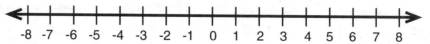

2. $y - 3 > 2$ _____

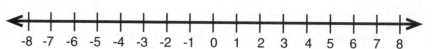

3. $7 + a \leq 3$ _____

4. $r - 6 < 0$ _____

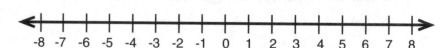

5. $s + 5 \geq 3$ _____

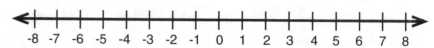

6. $t - 3 > -3$ _____

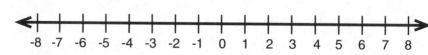

Equations & Inequalities (cont.)

ACTIVITY 77 Solving Inequalities by Dividing or Multiplying

Name:_____

Date:_____

Solve each inequality by dividing or multiplying. Then graph the solution.

1. $6q \geq 24$ _____

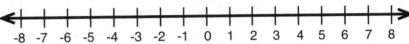

2. $5n < 15$ _____

3. $4c > -4$ _____

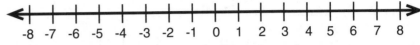

4. $\dfrac{x}{2} \leq 1$ _____

5. $\dfrac{s}{3} < 2$ _____

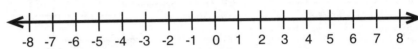

6. $\dfrac{y}{4} \geq -1$ _____

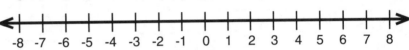

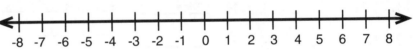

ACTIVITY 78 Review Solving Inequalities/Test Taking

Name:_____

Date:_____

Fill in the bubble next to the correct solution to each inequality.

1. $t - 7 < -4$ (a.) $t < -3$ (b.) $t < 3$ (c.) $t < -11$

2. $x + 3 \geq 5$ (a.) $x \geq 2$ (b.) $x \leq 2$ (c.) $x > 2$

3. $2b - 5 < 7$ (a.) $b < 6$ (b.) $b < 12$ (c.) $b \geq 6$

4. $\dfrac{w}{4} \leq 1$ (a.) $w \leq \dfrac{1}{4}$ (b.) $w \leq -3$ (c.) $w \leq 4$

5. $3(r + 1) > 0$ (a.) $r > 1$ (b.) $r > -3$ (c.) $r > -1$

6. $\dfrac{m}{2} + 6 < 9$ (a.) $m < 12$ (b.) $m < 6$ (c.) $m < \dfrac{3}{2}$

41

Graphing in the Coordinate Plane

ACTIVITY 79 Graphing in the
Coordinate Plane

Name:_____

Date:_____

Name the point at each coordinate.

1. (-2, -6) _____ **2.** (4, 4) _____

3. (3, -2) _____ **4.** (0, 5) _____

5. (-3, 3) _____ **6.** (1, -3) _____

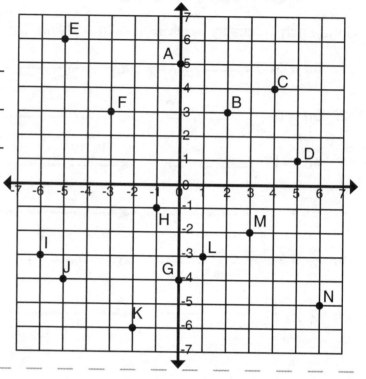

Give the coordinates for each point.

7. B _____ **8.** N _____

9. J _____ **10.** G _____

11. I _____ **12.** H _____

13. D _____ **14.** E _____

ACTIVITY 80 Graphing in the
Coordinate Plane

Name:_____

Date:_____

Draw this figure of a square inside a
square inside a square by plotting the
following points on the graph and then
connecting the sides of each square.

Largest square:
(-6, 6)   (6, 6)
(-6, -6)   (6, -6)

Middle square:
(-4, 4)   (4, 4)
(-4, -4)   (4, -4)

Smallest square:
(-2, 2)   (2, 2)
(-2, -2)   (2, -2)

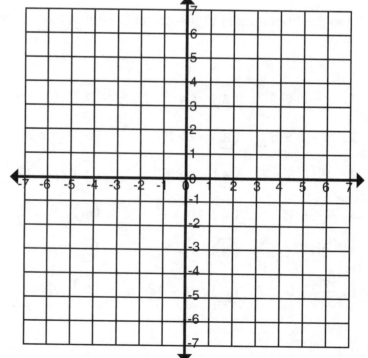

Graphing in the Coordinate Plane (cont.)

ACTIVITY 81 Equations With Two Variables

Name: _____

Date: _____

When the numbers in an ordered pair make an equation true, then that ordered pair is a solution of that equation.

Examples: Is (2, 6) a solution for the equation $x + y = 8$? Yes, because $2 + 6 = 8$ is true. What would be some other solutions for that equation? (4, 4); (3, 5); (6, 2); (-2, 10)

Write "yes" or "no" to indicate whether each ordered pair is a solution of the given equation.

$2x + y = 10$

1. (3, 4) _____
2. (4, 1) _____
3. (-5, 0) _____
4. (7, -8) _____
5. (-6, -6) _____
6. (4, -18) _____

What value of y in each ordered pair would make the equation true?

$4x - y = 10$

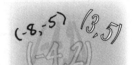

7. (5, ?) _____
8. (4, ?) _____
9. (3, ?) _____
10. (-1, ?) _____
11. (0, ?) _____
12. (1, ?) _____

(-8,-5) (3,5)
(-4,2)
(2,7) (9,-2)

ACTIVITY 82 Graphing Linear Equations

Name: _____

Date: _____

Complete the table of possible solutions for each equation and then graph the points and connect them to form a separate line for each equation.

1. $y = 3x - 4$

x	y
0	
-1	
2	
3	

2. $y = -x + 6$

x	y
4	
1	
0	
6	

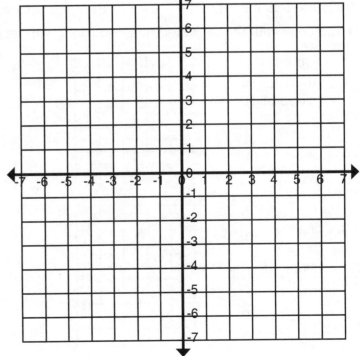

Graphing in the Coordinate Plane (cont.)

ACTIVITY 83 **Graphing Linear**
Equations

Name:_____

Date:_____

Graph each linear equation.

1. $y = -2x + 1$ 2. $y = 3x - 2$ 3. $y = \frac{1}{2}x + 1$ 4. $y = 3x$

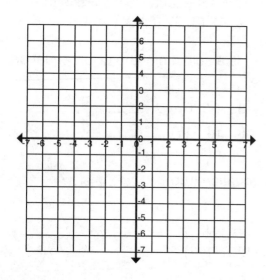
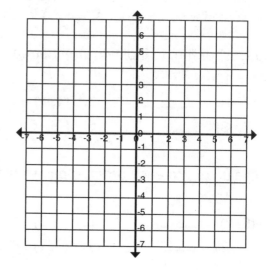

ACTIVITY 84 **Slope**

Name:_____

Date:_____

Reminder: The slope of a line is how steep it is. It is calculated as the ratio of $\frac{rise}{run}$. Start at the bottom left corner of the graph paper and make a staircase with the indicated rise and run. Then draw a line touching the tips of each stair.

1. rise = 1
   run = 1
   (slope of 1)

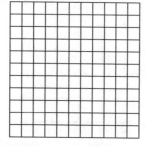

2. rise = 3
   run = 2
   (slope of $\frac{3}{2}$)

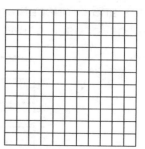

3. rise = 2
   run = 1
   (slope of $\frac{2}{1}$ = 2)

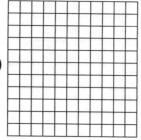

4. rise = 1
   run = 2
   (slope of $\frac{1}{2}$)

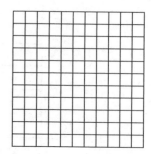

Graphing in the Coordinate Plane (cont.)

ACTIVITY 85 **Finding Slope From a Graph**

Name:_____

Date:_____

To find the slope of a line, choose two points on the line and count the rise and the run between those two points. Write them as a ratio (fraction). Find the slope of each line.

1. _____ 2. _____

3. _____ 4. _____

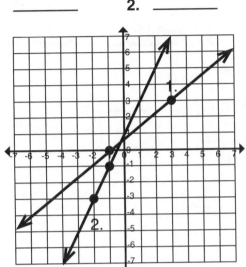

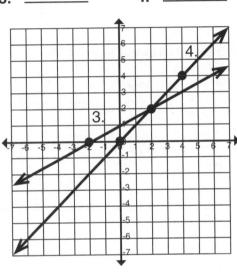

ACTIVITY 86 **Negative Slope and Zero Slope**

Name:_____

Date:_____

A line moving upward from left to right has a positive slope. A line moving downward from left to right has a negative slope. If a line is horizontal it has a zero slope. Find the slope of each line. Hint: all of these have negative slopes or zero slopes.

1. _____ 2. _____

3. _____ 4. _____

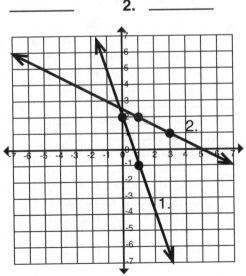

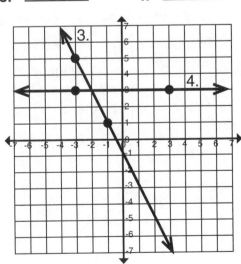

Graphing in the Coordinate Plane (cont.)

ACTIVITY 87 **Finding Slope Using Two Points**

Name: _____

Date: _____

You can find the slope of a line by subtracting the y coordinates and the x coordinates and putting them in a ratio: $\dfrac{y_2 - y_1}{x_2 - x_1}$.

Using the coordinates given, find the slope of each line.

1. (0, 3) and (3, 2) _____
2. (-1, 3) and (0, 0) _____

3. (-2, -1) and (2, 1) _____
4. (-3, 0) and (3, 2) _____

5. (-2, -2) and (2, 2) _____
6. (0, 1) and (2, 3) _____

ACTIVITY 88 **Graphing Linear Equations Using Slope**

Name: _____

Date: _____

You can graph a line if you know one point on that line and the slope. To do so, first plot the point. Then find other points on the line by moving up/down and over according to the rise and run indicated in the slope.

Example: If you know the point (2, 1) and the slope $\dfrac{1}{2}$, then you plot point (2, 1) and then go up one and over two to point (4, 2). Do another point by moving up one and over two from there to point (6, 3). Connect the points to show the line.

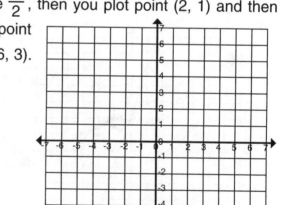

Graph the line that has the given point and slope.

1. (-1, -3), $\dfrac{2}{3}$

2. (0, 2), $-\dfrac{1}{2}$

3. (0, -4), $\dfrac{3}{2}$

Graphing in the Coordinate Plane (cont.)

ACTIVITY 89 Finding *x-* and *y-*
Intercepts

Name:_____

Date:_____

To find the *x*-intercept for a line, let $y = 0$ and solve for *x*. To find the *y*-intercept of a line, let $x = 0$ and solve for *y*.

Example: $y = x - 4$ If $y = 0$, then $0 = x - 4$. Add 4 to both sides and $4 = x$.
So one point on the line is (4, 0).
If $x = 0$, then $y = 0 - 4$, or $y = -4$.
So another point on the line is (0, -4).

You could then plot those two points and connect them to show the line.

Find the *x*- and *y*-intercepts to help you graph each line. Use your own graph paper.

1. $y = 2x + 2$

    x-intercept _____

    y-intercept _____

2. $y = -x + 1$

    x-intercept _____

    y-intercept _____

3. $y = 3x - 3$

    x-intercept _____

    y-intercept _____

ACTIVITY 90 **Equations in
Slope-Intercept Form**

Name:_____

Date:_____

When an equation is in the form $y = mx + b$, then *m* indicates the slope, and *b* indicates the *y*-intercept.

Example: $y = \frac{3}{4}x + 7$ The slope is $\frac{3}{4}$ and the *y*-intercept is 7.

Tell what the slope and *y*-intercept of each equation is.

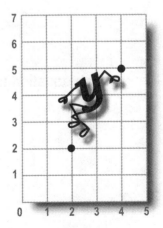

1. $y = \frac{1}{3}x - 6$ slope _____ *y*-intercept _____

2. $y = -3x + 4$ slope _____ *y*-intercept _____

3. $y = -\frac{2}{5}x - \frac{1}{2}$ slope _____ *y*-intercept _____

4. $y = 4x - 2$ slope _____ *y*-intercept _____

Graphing in the Coordinate Plane (cont.)

ACTIVITY 91 Writing an Equation
for a Line

Name:_____

Date:_____

Use the slope-intercept form ($y = mx + b$) to help write an equation for a line. First, find the y-intercept of the line, and then find the slope. Use that information to write an equation with the form $y = mx + b$.

1.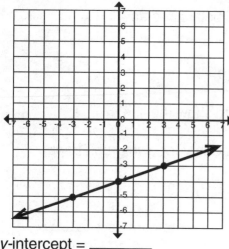

2.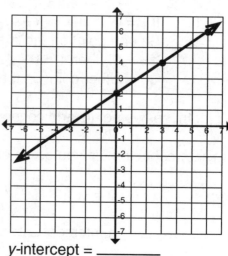

y-intercept = _____
Slope = _____
Equation of line _____

y-intercept = _____
Slope = _____
Equation of line _____

ACTIVITY 92 Changing Equations to
Slope-Intercept Form

Name:_____

Date:_____

Not all equations are written in slope-intercept form. You can change them to that form by isolating y on one side.

Example: $4x + 2y = 8$ Subtract $4x$ from both sides: $2y = 8 - 4x$

Divide both sides by 2: $\frac{2}{2}y = \frac{8}{2} - \frac{4}{2}x \longrightarrow y = 4 - 2x$

Rearrange the right side: $y = -2x + 4$ (slope-intercept form)

Change each equation to slope-intercept form.

1. $2x + 3y = 9$ _____

2. $3x + y = 6$ _____

3. $-x + 2y = 4$ _____

4. $5x - 4y = 12$ _____

48

Graphing in the Coordinate Plane (cont.)

ACTIVITY 93 **Review: Graphing Linear** Name:_____

Equations/Test Taking Date:_____

Use any method (making a table, point-slope, finding *x*- and *y*-intercepts, slope-intercept form) to graph and label each equation. Tell which method you used.

1. $y = 2x + 2$

   method: _____

2. $y = -\frac{1}{2}x - 1$

   method: _____

3. $4x + 2y = 6$

   method: _____

4. $y = \frac{1}{3}x + 3$

   method: _____

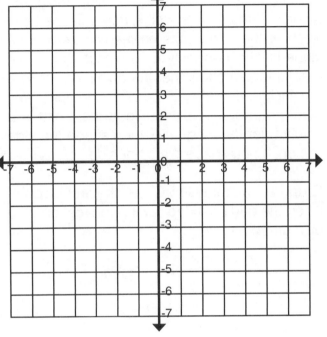

ACTIVITY 94 **Review Graphing Linear** Name:_____

Equations/Test Taking Date:_____

Mark the correct answer for each question.

1. What is the slope of the line $y = -\frac{2}{3}x - 1$?

   (a.) 5   (b.) $-\frac{2}{3}$ (c.) -2   (d.) $\frac{5}{3}$

2. What type of slope does a line going downward from left to right have?

   (a.) negative (b.) positive (c.) zero (d.) no slope

3. Which point is a solution for the equation $y = 2x + 3$?

   (a.) (3, 8)   (b.) (-2, 0)   (c.) (0, -5)   (d.) (2, 7)

4. What is the slope of the line that passes through points (0, 5) and (2, 7)?

   (a.) -1   (b.) 1   (c.) $\frac{1}{2}$ (d.) $-\frac{1}{2}$

49

Graphing in the Coordinate Plane (cont.)

ACTIVITY 95 **Graphing Inequalities**

Name:_____

Date:_____

Reminder: To graph an inequality, first change the inequality sign to an "equals" sign and graph the line. If the sign is < or >, use a dashed line to show that the points on the line are not included in the inequality. If the sign is ≤ or ≥, use a solid line to show that the points on the line are included in the inequality. Then pick any point on one side of the line. If that point is a solution for the inequality, then shade the side it is on. If not, shade the other side.

Graph each inequality. Graph the first inequality on the grid provided. Graph the rest on your own graph paper.

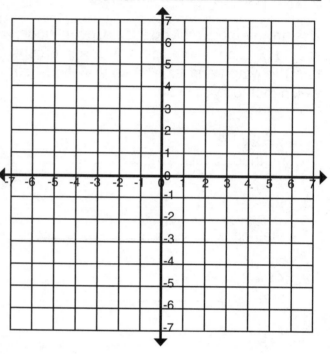

1. $y \leq x + 2$

2. $y > -2x - 2$

3. $y \geq \frac{1}{3}x - 1$

4. $y < x - 1$

ACTIVITY 96 **Systems of Linear Equations**

Name:_____

Date:_____

Reminder: The solution of a system of equations (two equations written together in the same problem) is the ordered pair that is a solution to both equations (or where the two lines they represent cross).

Tell the ordered pair that is the solution to each system of linear equations.

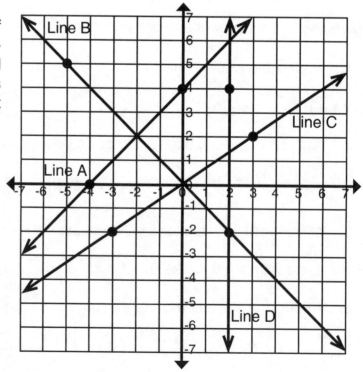

1. A and B _____

2. B and C _____

3. D and B _____

50

Graphing in the Coordinate Plane (cont.)

ACTIVITY 97 **Graphing Systems of Linear Equations**

Name:_____

Date:_____

Find the solution to these systems of linear equations by graphing both equations and finding where they intersect.

1. $y = x + 3$

$y = -3x - 1$

2. $y = 2x - 3$

$y = -2x + 1$

3. $y = \frac{1}{4}x + 3$

$y = 2x + 3$

solution: _____

solution: _____

solution: _____

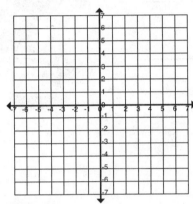
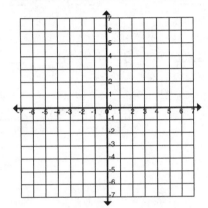
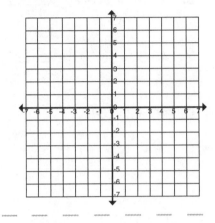

ACTIVITY 98 **Systems of Linear Equations With No Solution**

Name:_____

Date:_____

What type of lines would be needed so there is no solution to a system of equations?

_____

To find out, graph this system of linear equations that has no solution.

$y = x + 2$

$y = x - 3$

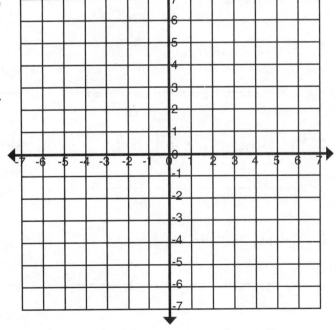

51

Ratios, Proportions, & Percents

ACTIVITY 99 Ratios

Name:_____

Date:_____

Write each ratio as a fraction in simplest form.

1. 24 to 6 _____

2. 35:70 _____

3. 9 out of 27 _____

4. 25 to 100 _____

5. 2 out of every 5 _____

6. 15:33 _____

7. 45:30 _____

8. 4 to 18 _____

9. 16 out of 26 _____

10. 2 to 100 _____

ACTIVITY 100 Rates

Name:_____

Date:_____

Express each ratio as a unit rate.

1. $20 for 5 tickets

2. $42 for 14 gallons of gas

_____

_____

3. 3.6 inches of rain in 12 hours

4. $8.50 for 10 pounds of apples

_____

_____

5. Driving 250 miles in 4 hours

6. $2.16 for 4 ounces of cereal

_____

_____

Ratios, Proportions, & Percents (cont.)

ACTIVITY 101 Equivalent Ratios

Name: _____

Date: _____

Reminder: To find equivalent ratios, multiply the numerator and the denominator by the same number (except 0).

List two equivalent ratios for each ratio.

1. $\dfrac{3}{4}$ _____

   _____

2. $\dfrac{1}{6}$ _____

   _____

3. $\dfrac{10}{12}$ _____

   _____

4. $\dfrac{4}{9}$ _____

   _____

5. $\dfrac{9}{10}$ _____

   _____

6. $\dfrac{2}{5}$ _____

   _____

ACTIVITY 102 Proportions

Name: _____

Date: _____

Reminder: A proportion is an equation that gives two equivalent ratios. The cross products of a proportion are always equal.

If $\dfrac{a}{b} = \dfrac{c}{d}$ then $a \cdot d = b \cdot c$.

Write *Yes* or *No* to indicate if each of these is a proportion.

1. $\dfrac{1}{2} = \dfrac{4}{8}$ _____

2. $\dfrac{6}{18} = \dfrac{3}{9}$ _____

3. $\dfrac{4}{5} = \dfrac{8}{12}$ _____

Solve each proportion.

4. $\dfrac{n}{8} = \dfrac{6}{24}$ _____

5. $\dfrac{60}{15} = \dfrac{x}{3}$ _____

6. $\dfrac{10}{100} = \dfrac{3}{m}$ _____

7. $\dfrac{16}{5} = \dfrac{20}{t}$ _____

8. $\dfrac{7}{s} = \dfrac{4}{8}$ _____

9. $\dfrac{k}{9} = \dfrac{14}{3}$ _____

Ratios, Proportions, & Percents (cont.)

ACTIVITY 103 Using Proportions

Name: _____

Date: _____

a proportion to help you solve each of these problems.
nder: Make sure the ratios are in the same order.

4 gumballs cost $1.00. How much do 20 gumballs cost? _____

You use 4 gallons of gas to drive 100 miles. How many miles could you drive on 12 gallons of gas? _____

3. On a trip you spent $42 on food for the first 3 days. At that rate, how much will your meals cost for 8 days? _____

4. Johanna typed 3 pages of her assignment in 5 minutes. At that rate, how many pages will she be able to type in 30 minutes? _____

ACTIVITY 104 Changing Percents to Fractions

Name: _____

Date: _____

Reminder: To change a percent to a fraction, write it as a fraction with the denominator 100, and then simplify the fraction.

Example: $25\% = \dfrac{25}{100} = \dfrac{1}{4}$

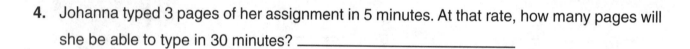

Change each of these percents to a fraction.

1. 15% _____

2. 20% _____

3. 32% _____

4. 125% _____

5. 100% _____

6. 50% _____

7. 66% _____

8. 70% _____

9. 60% _____

Ratios, Proportions, & Percents (cont.)

ACTIVITY 105 **Changing Percents to Decimals**

Name: _____

Date: _____

Reminder: To change percents to decimals, move the decimal point two places to the left and remove the percent sign.

Example: 67% = 0.67

Change each percent to a decimal.

1. 74% _____

2. 6% _____

3. 150% _____

4. 400% _____

5. 250% _____

6. 3.7% _____

7. 5% _____

8. 75% _____

9. 10% _____

10. 2.25% _____

11. 258% _____

12. 6.5% _____

ACTIVITY 106 **Changing Decimals to Percents**

Name: _____

Date: _____

Reminder: To change a decimal to a percent, move the decimal point two places to the right and add the percent sign.

Examples: 0.34 = 34%   6.7 = 670%

DECIMALS & PERCENTS

Change each decimal to a percent.

1. 0.5 _____

2. 0.67 _____

3. 0.59 _____

4. 0.03 _____

5. 0.7 _____

6. 2.5 _____

7. 6.0 _____

8. 0.09 _____

9. 0.8 _____

55

Ratios, Proportions, & Percents (cont.)

ACTIVITY 107 **Changing Fractions**
to Percents

Name:_____

Date:_____

Reminder: To change a fraction to a percent, first change the fraction to an equivalent fraction with a denominator of 100. The numerator is the percent—just add the sign.

Change each fraction to a percent.

1. $\frac{1}{2}$ _____

2. $\frac{2}{5}$ _____

3. $\frac{1}{4}$ _____

4. $\frac{4}{5}$ _____

5. $\frac{5}{2}$ _____

6. 2 _____

7. $\frac{3}{4}$ _____

8. $\frac{6}{10}$ _____

9. $\frac{15}{10}$ _____

- -

ACTIVITY 108 **Calculating Percents**
From a Graph

Name:_____

Date:_____

A math test had 24 questions. The tally graph shows how many questions each girl answered correctly. Use the graph to answer the questions.

1. What fraction of questions did Lisa answer correctly? _____ What percent is that? _____

2. What percent of the girls got at least 15 questions correct? _____

3. What percent of the girls got less than 15 questions correct? _____

4. What percent did Sari get wrong? _____

Number of Questions Answered Correctly	
Amy	𝍫𝍫𝍫 I
Jina	𝍫𝍫 IIII
Sari	𝍫𝍫 II
Lisa	𝍫𝍫𝍫 III
Mya	𝍫𝍫𝍫𝍫

Ratios, Proportions, & Percents (cont.)

ACTIVITY 109 **Percent Problems**

Name:_____

Date:_____

Reminder: The word *of* in mathematics means to multiply.
For problems that ask what number is a certain percent of a given number, change the percent to a decimal and then multiply by the number.

Example: What is 45% of 80? (0.45)(80) = ? 45% of 80 is 36.

Calculate these percentages.

1. What is 75% of 120? _____

2. What is 30% of 50? _____

3. What is 25% of 88? _____

4. What is 10% of 34? _____

5. What is 20% of 200? _____

6. What is 98% of 150? _____

7. What is 2% of 24? _____

8. What is 15% of 30? _____

ACTIVITY 110 **Percent Problems**

Name:_____

Date:_____

Reminder: The word *of* in mathematics means to multiply.
For problems that ask what percent of one number another number is, set up a proportion as in this example.

Example: 45 is what percent of 90? $\dfrac{45}{90} = \dfrac{p}{100}$

Cross multiply: Solve for 45 · 100 = 90*p*. Solve for *p* ⟶ $p = \dfrac{4,500}{90} = 50$, so 45 is 50% of 90.

Solve.

1. 25 is what percent of 50? _____

2. 60 is what percent of 180? _____

3. 12 is what percent of 60? _____

4. 100 is what percent of 1,000? _____

5. 18 is what percent of 360? _____

6. 75 is what percent of 300? _____

7. 14 is what percent of 70? _____

8. 35 is what percent of 140? _____

Ratios, Proportions, & Percents (cont.)

ACTIVITY 111 Percent Problems

Name:_____

Date:_____

Reminder: The word *of* in mathematics means to multiply.
To solve a problem that asks a certain percent of what number is another number, set up a problem like the one in the example.

Example: 80% of what number is 52? First change the percent to a decimal (80% = 0.8). Then call the unknown *n* and set up an equation: $(0.8)(n) = 52$. Solve the equation by dividing both sides by 0.8 $\longrightarrow$ $n = \dfrac{52}{0.8} = 65$, so 80% of 65 is 52.

Solve.

1. 75% of what number is 60? _____

2. 42% of what number is 63? _____

3. 20% of what number is 15? _____

4. 75% of what number is 48? _____

5. 60% of what number is 42? _____

6. 6% of what number is 12? _____

7. 9% of what number is 45? _____

8. 30% of what number is 15? _____

ACTIVITY 112 **Word Problems With Percents**

Name:_____

Date:_____

Solve.

1. Sam scored 85% on his test. There were 60 problems on the test. How many did he get right? _____

2. Lorisa is a waitress. Her customers' bills totaled $300. She earned $45 in tips. What percent did her customers tip her? _____

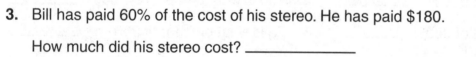

3. Bill has paid 60% of the cost of his stereo. He has paid $180. How much did his stereo cost? _____

4. How much does a $500 TV cost that is on sale for 25% off? _____

Ratios, Proportions, & Percents (cont.)

ACTIVITY 113 **Percent of Change**

Name:_____

Date:_____

Reminder: To find the percent of change, follow these steps:
- Subtract to find the amount of change.
- Divide the amount of change by the original amount.
- Change the decimal to a percent. Indicate if the change is positive or negative (going up or down).

Example: What is the percent of change from 100 pounds to 160 pounds?

$160 - 100 = 60 \longrightarrow \dfrac{60}{100} = 0.6 = 60\%$ increase

Find the percent of change. Indicate if each is an increase or a decrease. Round answers to the nearest tenth.

1. From 50 to 75 _____
2. From 32 to 8 _____
3. From 150 to 250 _____
4. From 80 to 160 _____
5. From 125 to 50 _____
6. From 145 to 0 _____
7. From 100 to 81 _____
8. From 16 to 20 _____

ACTIVITY 114 **Review Percents/ Test Taking**

Name:_____

Date:_____

Fill in the bubble next to the correct answer.

1. Change 20% to a fraction.   (a.) $\dfrac{1}{20}$ (b.) $\dfrac{1}{5}$ (c.) $\dfrac{1}{200}$

2. Change 7% to a decimal.   (a.) 0.7   (b.) 7.1   (c.) 0.07

3. Change 3.5 to a percent.   (a.) 35%   (b.) 350%   (c.) 3.5%

4. What is 30% of 60?   (a.) 18   (b.) 24   (c.) 30

5. 40 is what percent of 160?   (a.) 25%   (b.) 30%   (c.) 20%

6. 60% of what number is 90?   (a.) 100   (b.) 120   (c.) 150

Rational Numbers & Irrational Numbers

ACTIVITY 115 **Comparing Rational Numbers**

Name:_____

Date:_____

Reminder: To compare two rational numbers, write each so that they have the same positive denominator and then compare the numerators.

Example: $\frac{2}{3}$ ☐ $\frac{3}{4}$ The LCM of the denominators is 12, so rewrite each fraction with a

denominator of 12 ⟶ $\frac{8}{12}$ ☐ $\frac{9}{12}$. ⟶ Then compare numerators $\frac{8}{12}$ $\boxed{<}$ $\frac{9}{12}$, so $\frac{2}{3}$ $\boxed{<}$ $\frac{3}{4}$.

Write <, >, or = in each ☐ .

1. $\frac{3}{5}$ ☐ $\frac{2}{5}$

2. $\frac{4}{8}$ ☐ $\frac{2}{4}$

3. $-\frac{7}{4}$ ☐ $-\frac{5}{3}$

4. $\frac{7}{9}$ ☐ $\frac{5}{6}$

5. $-\frac{4}{5}$ ☐ $-\frac{3}{6}$

6. $\frac{4}{5}$ ☐ $\frac{4}{6}$

7. $\frac{18}{6}$ ☐ $\frac{18}{9}$

8. $\frac{1}{2}$ ☐ $\frac{1}{3}$

9. $\frac{1}{2}$ ☐ $\frac{4}{8}$

ACTIVITY 116 **Adding Rational Numbers**

Name:_____

Date:_____

Add these rational numbers and write in simplest form.

1. $\frac{5}{12} + \left(-\frac{5}{8}\right)$ _____

2. $\frac{1}{10} + \left(-\frac{2}{5}\right)$ _____

3. $\frac{3}{16} + \frac{7}{8}$ _____

4. $-\frac{3}{2} + \frac{3}{8}$ _____

5. $\frac{1}{6} + \left(-\frac{5}{9}\right)$ _____

6. $-\frac{1}{2} + \left(-\frac{1}{3}\right)$ _____

7. -2.6 + 4.5 _____

8. 3.9 + 6.4 _____

9. 23.7 + (-45.2) _____

10. 1.27 + 0.5 _____

11. 30.45 + (-14.3) _____

12. -9.9 + (-8.8) _____

Rational Numbers & Irrational Numbers (cont.)

ACTIVITY 117 **Subtracting Rational Numbers**

Name:_____

Date:_____

Subtract these rational numbers and write in simplest form.

1. $\dfrac{1}{4} - \dfrac{2}{5}$ _____

2. $\dfrac{2}{3} - \left(-\dfrac{1}{4}\right)$ _____

3. $4\dfrac{1}{2} - 7$ _____

4. $-\dfrac{1}{10} - \left(-\dfrac{2}{5}\right)$ _____

5. $\dfrac{11}{12} - \dfrac{5}{8}$ _____

6. $-\dfrac{3}{8} - \left(-\dfrac{1}{2}\right)$ _____

7. -6.2 – 4.1 _____

8. 55.4 – 33.6 _____

9. 121.1 – (-67.4) _____

10. 13.34 – 19.6 _____

11. -4.75 – (-3.23) _____

12. 47.5 – 45.7 _____

RATIONAL NUMBERS

ACTIVITY 118 **Multiplying Rational Numbers**

Name:_____

Date:_____

Multiply and write in simplest form.

1. $\dfrac{6}{5} \cdot \dfrac{5}{6}$ _____

2. $-\dfrac{1}{3} \cdot \dfrac{1}{2}$ _____

3. $\dfrac{5}{6} \cdot \left(-\dfrac{3}{4}\right)$ _____

4. $\dfrac{9}{10} \cdot \dfrac{5}{3}$ _____

5. $-\dfrac{7}{4} \cdot \left(-\dfrac{7}{4}\right)$ _____

6. $2\dfrac{2}{3} \cdot 4$ _____

7. 1.6 · 2.4 _____

8. -2.7 · 3.1 _____

9. -7.25 · (-3.3) _____

10. 7.8 · (-5) _____

11. 4.11 · 4.2 _____

12. -6 · 5.5 _____

Rational Numbers & Irrational Numbers (cont.)

ACTIVITY 119 Dividing Rational Numbers

Name:_____

Date:_____

Divide and write in simplest form.

1. $\frac{3}{4} \div \frac{1}{2}$ _____

2. $-\frac{3}{10} \div \frac{4}{5}$ _____

3. $-\frac{3}{4} \div \frac{1}{4}$ _____

4. $\frac{1}{2} \div \frac{1}{3}$ _____

5. $\frac{2}{3} \div \left(-\frac{1}{2}\right)$ _____

6. $\frac{5}{8} \div \frac{2}{3}$ _____

7. $18.4 \div 2$ _____

8. $-0.66 \div 0.3$ _____

9. $14 \div 2.2$ _____

10. $-1.8 \div (-1.2)$ _____

11. $3.25 \div 5$ _____

12. $100 \div (-0.25)$ _____

ACTIVITY 120 Solving Equations With Rational Numbers (+/-)

Name:_____

Date:_____

Solve each equation for x.

1. $3x + 8 = 13$ _____

2. $24 - 15x = 16$ _____

3. $4x - 3 = 9$ _____

4. $-15 - 6x = 15$ _____

5. $-7x - 16 = -12$ _____

6. $18 + 12x = -6$ _____

7. $-8 - 5x = 7$ _____

8. $9 + 7x = -3$ _____

Rational Numbers & Irrational Numbers (cont.)

ACTIVITY 121 **Solving Equations With Rational Numbers (· / ÷)**

Name:_____

Date:_____

Solve each equation for x.

1. $3.2x = 19.2$ _____

2. $\frac{2}{3}x = 9$ _____

3. $-5.4x = 16.2$ _____

4. $\frac{3}{4}x = -21$ _____

5. $\frac{x}{3.1} = 4$ _____

6. $\frac{x}{0.5} = 9$ _____

7. $\frac{-x}{7.25} = -2$ _____

8. $\frac{x}{2.2} = -2.2$ _____

ACTIVITY 122 **Solving Equations With Rational Numbers**

Name:_____

Date:_____

Solve each equation for x.

1. $x - 5x = 16$ _____

2. $4x + 10x = 28$ _____

3. $8x + 6 - 5x = 6$ _____

4. $12x - x + 5 = 6$ _____

5. $7x + 4x = 33$ _____

6. $7x + 2x - 5 = 0$ _____

7. $9x - x = -48$ _____

8. $-6x + 1 - 13x = -18$ _____

Rational Numbers & Irrational Numbers (cont.)

ACTIVITY 123 **Square Roots**

Name:_____

Date:_____

Reminder: Every positive number has two square roots. One is positive and one is negative.

Example: $x^2 = 9 \longrightarrow 3 \cdot 3 = 9$ and $-3 \cdot -3 = 9$. This is written as $x = \pm 3$.

Find two solutions for each equation.

1. $x^2 = 16$ _____

2. $b^2 = 25$ _____

3. $r^2 = 36$ _____

4. $d^2 = 100$ _____

5. $n^2 = 144$ _____

6. $h^2 = 64$ _____

7. $c^2 = 81$ _____

8. $t^2 = 400$ _____

ACTIVITY 124 **Square Roots**

Name:_____

Date:_____

Reminder: The symbol $\sqrt{}$ is used to indicate a nonnegative square root, and the symbol $-\sqrt{}$, is used to indicate a negative square root.

Find each square root indicated.

1. $\sqrt{49}$ _____

2. $\sqrt{121}$ _____

3. $\sqrt{1}$ _____

4. $\sqrt{169}$ _____

5. $-\sqrt{4}$ _____

6. $-\sqrt{225}$ _____

7. $-\sqrt{100}$ _____

8. $-\sqrt{196}$ _____

Rational Numbers & Irrational Numbers (cont.)

ACTIVITY 125 Adding and Subtracting Square Roots

Name:_____

Date:_____

Solve.

1. $\sqrt{81} - \sqrt{49}$ _____

2. $\sqrt{9} + \sqrt{16}$ _____

3. $\sqrt{121} - \sqrt{4}$ _____

4. $\sqrt{20 + 5}$ _____

5. $\sqrt{36} + \sqrt{64} + \sqrt{1}$ _____

6. $\sqrt{164 - 20}$ _____

7. $\sqrt{90 - 9} + \sqrt{54 - 5}$ _____

8. $\sqrt{9 + 7} - \sqrt{9 - 5}$ _____

ACTIVITY 126 Multiplying and Dividing Square Roots

Name:_____

Date:_____

Solve.

1. $5 \cdot \sqrt{25}$ _____

2. $36 \div \sqrt{16}$ _____

3. $\sqrt{100} \cdot \sqrt{49}$ _____

4. $\sqrt{4 \cdot 16}$ _____

5. $\sqrt{144} \div \sqrt{4}$ _____

6. $\sqrt{9} \cdot \sqrt{4} \cdot \sqrt{49}$ _____

7. $(\sqrt{64} \cdot \sqrt{16}) \div \sqrt{4}$ _____

8. $\sqrt{25} \cdot (-\sqrt{121})$ _____

Rational Numbers & Irrational Numbers (cont.)

ACTIVITY 127 Approximate
Square Roots

Name:_____

Date:_____

Reminder: If a number is not a perfect square, you can estimate the square root by finding the two perfect squares just less than and just greater than the number and seeing which is closer.

> **Example:** 44 is not a perfect square. It is greater than 36 (6^2) and less than 49 (7^2).
> 44 is closer to 49, so the closest estimate for $\sqrt{44}$ would be 7.

Find the best whole number estimate for each square root.

1. $\sqrt{83}$ 2. $\sqrt{19}$ 3. $\sqrt{96}$ 4. $\sqrt{47}$

_____   _____   _____   _____

LOW

5. $-\sqrt{56}$ 6. $-\sqrt{12}$ 7. $-\sqrt{99}$ 8. $-\sqrt{2}$

_____   _____   _____   _____

HIGH

ACTIVITY 128 **Square Roots and**
Rational Numbers

Name:_____

Date:_____

Reminder: To find the square root of a fraction, find the square root of the numerator and the square root of the denominator and simplify if necessary.

$$\sqrt{\frac{64}{16}}$$

Solve.

1. $\sqrt{\dfrac{9}{16}}$ _____   2. $\sqrt{\dfrac{64}{16}}$ _____

3. $-\sqrt{\dfrac{4}{36}}$ _____   4. $\sqrt{\dfrac{49}{81}}$ _____

5. $\sqrt{\dfrac{144}{121}}$ _____   6. $-\sqrt{\dfrac{25}{100}}$ _____

7. $-\sqrt{\dfrac{169}{225}}$ _____   8. $\sqrt{\dfrac{36}{144}}$ _____

Rational Numbers & Irrational Numbers (cont.)

ACTIVITY 129 **Review Square Roots/**   Name:_____
Test Taking   Date:_____

Fill in the bubble next to the correct answer.

1. $\sqrt{81}$ (a.) 8   (b.) 9   (c.) 7

2. $-\sqrt{49}$ (a.) -7   (b.) 7   (c.) -8

3. Estimated $\sqrt{70}$ (a.) 8   (b.) 9   (c.) 10

4. $\sqrt{16} + \sqrt{25}$ (a.) $\sqrt{41}$ (b.) 8   (c.) 9

5. $-\sqrt{80 - 16}$ (a.) -64   (b.) -16   (c.) -8

6. Estimated $-\sqrt{13}$ (a.) -4   (b.) -3   (c.) -5

ACTIVITY 130 **Review Square Roots/**   Name:_____
Test Taking   Date:_____

Fill in the bubble next to the correct answer.

1. $\sqrt{9} \cdot \sqrt{25}$ (a.) 34   (b.) 8   (c.) 15

2. $\sqrt{48 \cdot 3}$ (a.) 12   (b.) 13   (c.) 14

3. $\sqrt{100} \div \sqrt{25}$ (a.) 4   (b.) 2   (c.) 5

4. $\sqrt{98 \div 2}$ (a.) 7   (b.) 6   (c.) 8

5. $-\sqrt{\dfrac{36}{81}}$ (a.) $-\dfrac{1}{3}$ (b.) $-\dfrac{2}{3}$ (c.) $-\dfrac{6}{3}$

6. $\sqrt{\dfrac{121}{64}}$ (a.) $1\dfrac{3}{8}$ (b.) 14   (c.) $\dfrac{8}{11}$

Rational Numbers & Irrational Numbers (cont.)

ACTIVITY 131 Square Roots and Equations

Name:_____

Date:_____

Reminder: To solve equations with squared variables, isolate the squared variable and use the square root to solve for its root.

> **Example:** $y^2 + 3 = 28$
> Subtract 3 from both sides to get $y^2 = 25$,
> then take the square root of both sides. $\sqrt{y^2} = \sqrt{25} \longrightarrow y = 5$

Find the positive solution to each equation.

1. $c^2 - 6 = 30$ _____

2. $m^2 + 7 = 56$ _____

3. $a^2 - 2 = 14$ _____

4. $z^2 + 4 = 68$ _____

5. $b^2 + 9 = 90$ _____

6. $h^2 - 10 = 90$ _____

7. $f^2 + 2 = 27$ _____

8. $y^2 - 4 = 5$ _____

ACTIVITY 132 The Pythagorean Theorem

Name:_____

Date:_____

The **Pythagorean Theorem** is $a^2 + b^2 = c^2$ (where a and b are the lengths of the two legs of a right triangle and c is the length of the hypotenuse of a right triangle). If you know the lengths of two of the sides, you can plug them into the formula and solve for the unknown side.

Find the length of the unknown side of each right triangle below.

1. _____
   $a = 3$ $c = ?$ $b = 4$

2. _____
   $c = ?$ $b = 8$ $a = 15$

3. _____
   $c = 13$ $a = 5$ $b = ?$

4. _____
   $a = ?$ $c = 10$ $b = 6$

5. _____
   $c = 20$ $b = ?$ $a = 12$

6. _____
   $a = 15$ $c = ?$ $b = 20$

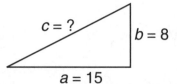

Rational Numbers & Irrational Numbers (cont.)

ACTIVITY 133 Using the Pythagorean Theorem

Name:_____

Date:_____

Use the Pythagorean Theorem ($a^2 + b^2 = c^2$) to help you solve each of these problems. Use a calculator and round to the nearest tenth.

1. A 10-foot tree casts a shadow 12 feet long on the ground. How far would it be from the top of the tree to the tip of its shadow?

   _____

2. A TV has a diagonal of 25 inches. It is 15 inches tall. How wide is it?

   _____

3. A square has sides 6 inches long. How long is its diagonal?

   _____

4. A 15-foot rope is tied to the top of a 9 foot pole. If you stretch the rope out tight and stake it into the ground, how far will the stake be from the pole?

   _____

ACTIVITY 134 Square Roots and Formulas

Name:_____

Date:_____

The formula to find the area of a circle is πr^2. The area of a circle is written as cm² (or in.²). Use 3.14 as the value of π to help you find the missing information. Use a calculator to help you. Round answers to the nearest hundredth.

Reminder: The diameter of a circle is twice as long as its radius.

1. If a circle has a radius of 4 centimeters (cm), what is the area of the circle?

   _____

2. If a circle has a diameter of 16 cm, what is the area of the circle?

   _____

3. If a circle has an area of 314 cm², how long is the radius?

   _____

4. If a circle has an area of 1,256 cm², how long is the diameter?

   _____

Polynomials

ACTIVITY 135 Polynomials

Name: _____

Date: _____

Tell whether each polynomial is a monomial, a binomial, or a trinomial.

1. $6m + 2n$ _____

2. $8h^2$ _____

3. $b^2 + 3b + 4$ _____

4. $xy^2 + 2x + 4$ _____

5. $4g$ _____

6. $8t^2 - 5$ _____

7. $j^2 - 3j - 4$ _____

8. cd _____

9. $w - 5$ _____

10. $r^2 + 6r - 7$ _____

ACTIVITY 136 Evaluating Polynomials

Name: _____

Date: _____

Evaluate each polynomial for $x = 1$, $y = 2$, and $z = -2$

1. $x^2 + y$ _____

2. $y^2 + z$ _____

3. $3xy$ _____

4. $x^2 + z^2$ _____

5. $2x + 2y + z$ _____

6. xyz _____

7. $x + 3y + 4z$ _____

8. $y^2 + z^2 - x$ _____

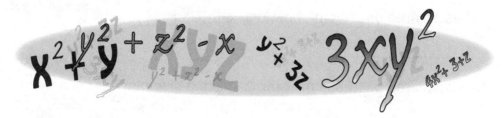

Polynomials (cont.)

ACTIVITY 137 Combining Like
Terms in Polynomials

Name:_____

Date:_____

Reminder: A coefficient is the numerical part of a monomial (**Example**: In $3xy$, the coefficient is 3). Like terms are either the same or only differ in coefficients.

Give the coefficients of a and b in each expression.

1. $2a + 4b$ _____

2. $-3a - 6b$ _____

3. $10a + b$ _____

Simplify by combining like terms.

4. $2x + 4y + 3x + 7y$

5. $n - 2m + 5n + 3m$

6. $4r^2 + r + 3r - 2r^2 + 1$

7. $g^3 + 4g^2 + 5g - 2g^2 + 2g^3$

8. $6c^2d - 5cd + 4cd - 3c^2d$

9. $w^4 - v^3 + 2w^3 + 3v^3 - 4w^4$

ACTIVITY 138 Adding Polynomials

Name:_____

Date:_____

To add polynomials, combine all of the like terms from each addend into one polynomial.

Add.

1. $(3c + 3) + (-6c + 8)$

2. $(6r + 5s + 7t) + (5r + 2t)$

3. $(4x + 6) + (2x + 7)$

4. $(9a^2 - b) + (2a^2 - 2b)$

5. $(3x^2 + 2x) + (4x^2 - 3x)$

6. $(3r + 2s) + (2r + s)$

7. $(3x^2 + 3x) + (2x^2 + 4x)$

8. $(a^2 + b^2) + (2a^2 + 2b^2)$

Polynomials (cont.)

ACTIVITY 139 **Problem Solving**
With Addition of Polynomials

Name:_____

Date:_____

Add polynomials to find the perimeter of each figure.

1.

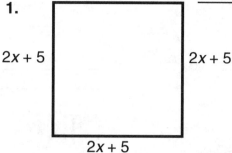

2x + 5

2x + 5   2x + 5

2x + 5

_____

2.

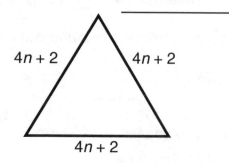

4n + 2   4n + 2

4n + 2

_____

3.

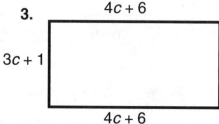

4c + 6

3c + 1   3c + 1

4c + 6

_____

ACTIVITY 140 **Subtracting**
Polynomials

Name:_____

Date:_____

To subtract a polynomial, add the opposite of the polynomial.

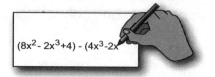

Subtract.

1. $(3g^2 + 5g) - (g^2 + 2g)$

_____

2. $(5x + 3y) - (3x + 2y)$

_____

3. $(2b^2 + 4b) - (b^2 + 2b)$

_____

4. $(3w + 5v) - (4w + 5v)$

_____

5. $(2r^2 - 3s) - (r^2 - 4s)$

_____

6. $(5e + 4f) - (2e - 3f)$

_____

7. $(6d^2 + 4e) - (3d^2 + e)$

_____

8. $(7m^2 - 4n) - (3m^2 - 2n)$

_____

Polynomials (cont.)

ACTIVITY 141 **Multiplying Monomials**

Name: _____

Date: _____

To multiply monomials, first multiply the coefficients. To multiply the variables, add their exponents.

Multiply.

1. $a^2 \cdot a^5$

_____

2. $3(4t)$

_____

3. $(3x)(2x)$

_____

4. $(-4)(3b)$

_____

5. $(2m^2)(-3n)$

_____

6. $(-3g)(2g^3)(4g^2)$

_____

7. $(-3s)(-3s)(-3s)$

_____

8. $(k^4)(2k^2)(-3k)$

_____

ACTIVITY 142 **Powers of Monomials**

Name: _____

Date: _____

To find the power of a power, multiply the exponents.

Simplify.

1. $(2^2)^2$

_____

2. $(-4x^3)^2$

_____

3. $(-5bc)^3$

_____

4. $(r^3)^{-2}$

_____

5. $(fg^2)^6$

_____

6. $(y^3z)^2$

_____

7. $(j^5)^3$

_____

8. $(a^2b^2c^2)^3$

_____

Polynomials (cont.)

ACTIVITY 143 Multiplying Polynomials by Monomials

Name:_____

Date:_____

Use the distributive property to help you multiply a polynomial by a monomial.

Example: $2x(x + 2) \longrightarrow 2x(x) + 2x(2) \longrightarrow 2x^2 + 4x$

Multiply.

1. $5(n + 4)$

_____

2. $3a(a + 5)$

_____

3. $5t(t + 3)$

_____

4. $3b(b + 2)$

_____

5. $2m(3n + p)$

_____

6. $3x(6x + 2y)$

_____

7. $3r(2r + 3s + 4t)$

_____

8. $5k(k - 2j - 7p)$

_____

ACTIVITY 144 Evaluating Products of Polynomials and Monomials

Name:_____

Date:_____

Evaluate each expression for $x = 2$, $y = 3$.

1. $2(x + 4)$

_____

2. $3(y + 2)$

_____

3. $3(x + y)$

_____

4. $x(x + 3)$

_____

5. $2x(x + y)$

_____

6. $x(x + y)$

_____

7. $2y(2x - 2y)$

_____

8. $3x(2 + 4y)$

_____

Polynomials (cont.)

ACTIVITY 145 **Dividing Polynomials**   Name:_____

by Monomials   Date:_____

To divide a polynomial by a monomial, divide each term of the polynomial by the monomial.

Example: $\dfrac{12x + 4}{4}$ $\longrightarrow$ $\dfrac{12x}{4} + \dfrac{4}{4}$ $\longrightarrow$ $3x + 1$

Divide.

1. $\dfrac{18n^2 + 6}{6}$ _____

2. $\dfrac{8b + 2}{2}$ _____

3. $\dfrac{21t^2 + 7t}{7t}$ _____

4. $\dfrac{m^2 + m}{m}$ _____

5. $\dfrac{20a^2 + 10a}{5a}$ _____

6. $\dfrac{y^3 + y^2}{y}$ _____

ACTIVITY 146 **Multiplying Binomials**   Name:_____

Date:_____

To multiply two binomials, multiply each term of the first binomial by each term of the second binomial using the distributive property.

Example: $(x + 3)(x + 4)$ $\longrightarrow$ $x(x + 4) + 3(x + 4)$ $\longrightarrow$ $x^2 + 4x + 3x + 12$ $\longrightarrow$ $x^2 + 7x + 12$

Multiply.

1. $(n + 4)(n + 5)$

_____

2. $(3b - 4)(2b - 6)$

_____

3. $(4t + 1)(t - 5)$

_____

4. $(x - 9)(x - 9)$

_____

5. $(2g + 4)(g - 2)$

_____

6. $(3a + 4)(2a - 5)$

_____

B I N O M I A L S

Polynomials (cont.)

ACTIVITY 147 **Problem Solving**
Using Polynomials

Name:_____

Date:_____

Write an equation to help you find the area of each rectangular prism. Remember, the area of a rectangular prism will be the length · width · height. Then simplify the expression.

1. length = x
   width = x
   height = 4

2. length = 3
   width = y
   height = $y + 4$

3. length = 5
   width = z
   height = $z + 5$

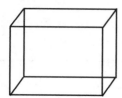

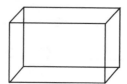

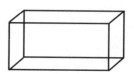

_____

_____

_____

ACTIVITY 148 **Problem Solving**
Using Polynomials

Name:_____

Date:_____

Use the signpost to help you solve the problems.

Jasper (7x +3) miles
Southbend (4x +2) miles
Noorland (3x +4) miles
Sunville (5x +6) miles

1. Which city is $(2x - 3)$ miles from Sunville?

   _____

2. Which city is $(3x + 1)$ miles from Jasper?

   _____

3. Which city is $(2x + 2)$ miles from Noorland?

   _____

4. If x is 40, how many miles is it from Noorland to Jasper?

   _____

Daily Skill Builders: Pre-Algebra

Polynomials

Polynomials (cont.)

ACTIVITY 149 **Problem Solving With**   Name:_____

Polynomials   Date:_____

Decide which of these equations would be used to solve each problem. Then solve the problem.

a. $x + (x - 12) + 2x = 92$ **b.** $x + (x + 12) + 2(x + 12) = 92$ **c.** $x + (x + 12) + 2x = 92$

1. Jaira earned $12 more selling candy bars on Tuesday than she earned on Monday. On Wednesday she earned twice what she earned on Monday. She earned $92 in all. How much did she earn on Monday? _____ _____

2. Steve earned $12 less selling candy bars on Tuesday than he did on Monday. On Wednesday he earned twice as much as he did on Monday. He earned $92 in all. How much did he earn on Monday? _____ _____

3. Pedro earned $12 more selling candy bars on Tuesday than he did on Monday. On Wednesday he earned twice what he earned on Tuesday. He earned $92 in all. How much did he earn on Monday? _____ _____

- -

ACTIVITY 150 **Problem Solving With**   Name:_____

Polynomials   Date:_____

Write an equation to help you solve each problem. Use *n* for nickels, *d* for dimes, and *q* for quarters.

Example: Eight coins (dimes and nickels) are worth 70 cents. How many of each are there? Since dimes are worth 10 cents and nickels are worth 5 cents, you can write this equation to solve the problem: $10d + 5(8 - d) = 70 \longrightarrow 10d + 40 - 5d = 70 \longrightarrow 5d + 40 = 70 \longrightarrow 5d = 30 \longrightarrow d = 6$. There are 6 dimes and $(8 - 6)$, or 2, nickels.

1. Twelve coins (dimes and nickels) are worth 90 cents. How many of each are there?

_____

2. Seven coins (quarters and nickels) are worth 75 cents. How many of each are there?

_____

3. Six coins (dimes and quarters) are worth 90 cents. How many of each are there?

_____

4. Nine coins (dimes and nickels) are worth 70 cents. How many of each are there?

_____

© Mark Twain Media, Inc., Publishers   77

Polynomials (cont.)

ACTIVITY 151 **Reviewing Adding and** Name:_____
Subtracting Polynomials/Test Taking Date:_____

Fill in the bubble next to the correct answer.

1. $(4x + 3y) + (2x + y)$
   - (a.) $7x + 3y$
   - (b.) $6x + 4y$
   - (c.) $6x + 2y$

2. $(5b - 2c) + (b + 4c)$
   - (a.) $6b + 2c$
   - (b.) $6b - 2c$
   - (c.) $4b - 2c$

3. $(-3r + 2s) + (-4r - 5s)$
   - (a.) $-7r - 3s$
   - (b.) $7r - 3s$
   - (c.) $r + 7s$

4. $(6e + 6f) - (3e + f)$
   - (a.) $3e + 7f$
   - (b.) $9e + 7f$
   - (c.) $3e + 5f$

5. $(2v^2 - 4w) - (v^2 + 3w)$
   - (a.) $v^2 - w$
   - (b.) $v^2 - 7w$
   - (c.) $3v^2 - w$

6. $(-3m^2 + 6n) - (2m^2 - 4n)$
   - (a.) $5m^2 + 2n$
   - (b.) $-5m^2 + 2n$
   - (c.) $-5m^2 + 10n$

ACTIVITY 152 **Reviewing Multiplying** Name:_____
and Dividing Polynomials/Test Taking Date:_____

Fill in the bubble next to the correct answer

1. $c^2 \cdot c^3$
   - (a.) c^5
   - (b.) c^6
   - (c.) c^{23}

2. $(-2xy)^3$
   - (a.) $6xy^3$
   - (b.) $-8xy^3$
   - (c.) $-8x^3y^3$

3. $2(b^3)(4b^4)$
   - (a.) $8b^7$
   - (b.) $8b^{12}$
   - (c.) $6b^7$

4. $\dfrac{15x + 10}{5}$
   - (a.) $5x + 5$
   - (b.) $3x + 2$
   - (c.) $10x + 5$

5. $\dfrac{9r^2 + 6}{3}$
   - (a.) $6r + 3$
   - (b.) $3r^2 + 2$
   - (c.) $3r^2 + 3$

6. $\dfrac{8m^2 + 4m}{4}$
   - (a.) $2m + 1$
   - (b.) $2m^2 + 4m$
   - (c.) $2m^2 + m$

Probability and Odds

ACTIVITY 153 Patterns and
Sequences

Name:_____

Date:_____

Write a rule to describe each sequence. Then find the next three terms in the sequence.

1. 10, 8, 6, 4,... _____

_____

2. 100, 125, 150, 175, 200,... _____

_____

3. 3.3, 3.6, 3.9, 4.2,... _____

_____

4. 4, 12, 36, 108,... _____

5. 940, 94, 9.4, 0.94,... _____

_____

6. $\frac{1}{2}, \frac{1}{4}, \frac{1}{8}, \frac{1}{16}$ .... _____

_____

ACTIVITY 154 Patterns and
Sequences

Name:_____

Date:_____

Decide which algebraic equation describes each sequence. Then find the next term in the sequence.

A. $x^2 - x$ 　　 B. $2x + 1$ 　　 C. $x(x + 1)$ 　　 D. $3x - 1$ 　　 E. x^2

1. _____ 3, 7, 15, 31,... _____

2. _____ 5, 14, 41, 122,... _____

3. _____ 2, 4, 16, 256,... _____

4. _____ 2; 6; 42; 1,806;... _____

5. _____ 3, 6, 30, 870,... _____

Probability and Odds (cont.)

ACTIVITY 155 **The Counting Principle** Name:_____

Date:_____

Find the number of possible outcomes for each situation.

1. There are 3 flavors of ice cream and 2 types of cones. How many types of one-dip ice cream cones are there to choose? _____

2. A shirt comes in short or long sleeves, 3 different colors, and 2 different types of fabric. How many possible combinations for the shirt are there? _____

3. At a restaurant you can choose from 4 different entrees, 3 different vegetables, 3 types of salads, and 2 kinds of bread. How many different meal combinations are there? _____

4. You can buy a car in 6 different exterior colors, 3 different interior colors, and either manual or automatic shift. How many different choices would you have? _____

ACTIVITY 156 **Factorials** Name:_____

Date:_____

Find the value of each factorial.

1. 7! _____

2. 10! _____

3. $\dfrac{10!}{8!}$ _____

4. $\dfrac{12!}{6!}$ _____

5. 9! – 5! _____

6. 2! · 2! _____

7. $\dfrac{5!3!}{3!4!}$ _____

8. $\dfrac{7!2!}{2!5!}$ _____

Probability and Odds (cont.)

ACTIVITY 157 **Probability**

Name:_____

Date:_____

Reminder: To find the probability of a particular event occurring, write the ratio of the number of ways the event can occur over the number of possible outcomes.

Example: The probability of rolling a 2 on a die is $\frac{1}{6}$ because there is only one way to roll a 2, and there are 6 possible outcomes when you roll a die.

If you roll a die one time, what is the probability that you will roll ...

1. The number 5 _____

2. An even number _____

3. A number less than 5 _____

4. A prime number _____

5. A 1 or a 3 _____

6. The number 9 _____

7. A factor of 12 _____

8. Not 3 _____

ACTIVITY 158 **Independent and Dependent Events**

Name:_____

Date:_____

Reminder: Two events are independent if the outcome of one does not affect the outcome of the other. They are dependent if the outcome of one does affect the outcome of the other.

Write *I* if the event is independent and *D* if it is dependent.

1. _____ Picking a card from a deck, not replacing it, and then picking another card.

2. _____ Eating an item from a tray of snacks, then choosing another item.

3. _____ Rolling a die, and then rolling it again.

4. _____ Choosing a hat from a rack of hats, then choosing a pair of shoes from a rack of shoes.

5. _____ Choosing a marble from a bag, replacing it, and then choosing another marble.

6. _____ Choosing a book from the shelf, not replacing it, and then choosing another book.

Probability and Odds (cont.)

ACTIVITY 159 Computing the
Probabilities of Two or More
Independent Events

Name: _____

Date: _____

Reminder: To compute the probability of two or more independent events, multiply the probability of the first event by the probability of the second event.

Example: What is the probability of rolling a 6 on a die and getting heads in a coin toss?

The probability of rolling the number 6 is $\frac{1}{6}$. The probability of getting heads is

$\frac{1}{2}$. The probability of rolling a 6 and getting heads is $\frac{1}{6} \cdot \frac{1}{2} = \frac{1}{12}$.

Calculate each probability for having a green die and a blue die. Put answers in simplest form.

1. green 3 and blue 6

_____

2. green even and blue even

_____

3. green even and blue odd

_____

4. green 1 and blue odd

_____

5. green prime and blue 6

_____

6. green factor of 6 and blue factor of 12

_____

ACTIVITY 160 **Odds**

Name: _____

Date: _____

Reminder: To find the odds in favor of an event occurring, write the ratio of the number of ways the event can occur to the number of ways that the event cannot occur. Simplify.

Example: What are the odds of choosing a black marble from a bag of 3 black marbles, 12 white marbles, and 5 red marbles? There are 3 chances of choosing a black and

17 chances of getting something other than a black. Write the ratio as $\frac{3}{17}$. The

odds are 3 to 17 of getting a black marble.

A gumball machine has 50 red balls, 40 blue balls, 35 yellow balls, and 25 white balls. Calculate the odds in favor of getting ...

1. A blue gumball

_____

2. A red or yellow gumball

_____

3. A color other than red

_____

4. A blue or white gumball

_____

5. A color from the US flag

_____

6. A color other than yellow or white

_____

Probability and Odds (cont.)

ACTIVITY 161 **Using a Sample to**   Name:_____

Make Predictions   Date:_____

Round answers to the nearest whole number.

1. In a sample, 20 out of 60 people said their favorite color was red. Based on the sample, how many people out of 900 would you predict like red the best? _____

2. In a sample, 25 out of 50 children said they prefer cheese piz-za to pepperoni. Based on the sample, how many children out of 300 would you predict prefer cheese pizza to pepperoni?
   _____

3. In a sample, 22 out of 30 people said that vanilla was their favorite flavor of ice cream. Based on the sample, how many people out of 100 would you predict like vanilla ice cream the best? _____

4. In a sample, 24 out of 30 people say they have taken the bus in the past month. Based on the sample, how many people out of 200 would you predict have taken the bus in the past month? _____

ACTIVITY 162 **Using a Sample to**   Name:_____

Make Decisions   Date:_____

A company makes basketballs. A worker inspects the balls before they are shipped. He inspects 600 balls and finds that 12 of them are defective. He talks to the manager, and they decide to change the speed at which the balls are glued. After the change, the worker inspects 1,000 balls and 15 are defective.

1. What percent of the balls were defective before the change? _____

2. What percent are defective after the change?_____

3. Did the change help improve the process? _____

 4. If the company makes 8,000 balls per week, how many would you expect to be defective per week (after the change)? _____

      83

Answer Keys

Activity 1 (page 3)
1. yes   **2.** no   **3.** no   **4.** yes   **5.** no   **6.** yes
7. 2, 4   **8.** 2, 5, 10   **9.** 1, 17   **10.** 2, 5, 8, 10
11. 2, 4, 8   **12.** 6, 8   **13.** 5, 25   **14.** 3, 5, 10, 15

Activity 2 (page 3)
1. 1, 2, 3, 4, 6, 8, 12, 24
2. 1, 2, 3, 5, 6, 10, 15, 30
3. 1, 2, 3, 6, 9, 18   **4.** 1, 5, 25
5. 1, 2, 3, 4, 6, 9, 12, 18, 36   **6.** 1, 3, 5, 9, 15, 45
7. 1, 2, 4, 5, 8, 10, 20, 40   **8.** 1, 29
9. 1, 3, 7, 21   **10.** 1, 2, 3, 4, 6, 12

Activity 3 (page 4)
Divisible by 2: 8, 10, 30, 36, 52, 484
Divisible by 3: 9, 27, 33, 24, 18, 423, 780
Divisible by 5: 35, 70, 90, 85, 110, 895
Divisible by 10: 80, 60, 20, 70, 220, 350
Bonus: 36

Activity 4 (page 4)
The following numbers should be circled: 2, 3, 5, 7, 11, 13, 17, 19, 23, 29, 31, 37, 41, 43, 47. The rest of the numbers should be underlined.

Activity 5 (page 5)
1. $2 \cdot 2 \cdot 11$ **2.** $2 \cdot 2 \cdot 2 \cdot 2 \cdot 2$ **3.** $3 \cdot 3 \cdot 5$
4. $2 \cdot 3 \cdot 3$ **5.** $2 \cdot 5 \cdot 5$ **6.** $2 \cdot 2 \cdot 7$

Activity 6 (page 5)
1. Factors of 20: 1, 2, 4, 5, 10, 20
Factors of 36: 1, 2, 3, 4, 6, 9, 12, 18, 36
Common Factors: 1, 2, 4   GCF: 4
2. Factors of 21: 1, 3, 7, 21
Factors of 28: 1, 2, 4, 7, 14, 28
Common Factors: 1, 7   GCF: 7
3. Factors of 16; 1, 2, 4, 8, 16
Factors of 42: 1, 2, 3, 6, 7, 14, 21, 42
Common Factors: 1, 2   GCF: 2
4. Factors of 24: 1, 2, 3, 4, 6, 8, 12, 24
Factors of 48: 1, 2, 3, 4, 6, 8, 12, 24, 48
Common Factors: 1, 2, 3, 4, 6, 8, 12, 24 GCF: 24

Activity 7 (page 6)
1. Prime factors of 12: 2, 3
Prime factors of 30: 2, 3, 5
Prime factors in common: 2, 3   GCF: 6
2. Prime factors of 21: 3, 7
Prime factors of 35: 5, 7
Prime factors in common: 7   GCF: 7
3. Prime factors of 18: 2, 3
Prime factors of 24: 2, 3
Prime factors in common: 2, 3   GCF: 6

4. Prime factors of 15: 3, 5
Prime factors of 50: 2, 5
Prime factors in common: 5   GCF: 5

Activity 8 (page 6)
1. Multiples of 4: 4, 8, 12, 16, 20, 24
Multiples of 6: 6, 12, 18, 24   LCM: 12
2. Multiples of 2: 2, 4, 6, 8, 10, 12, 14, 16, 18, 20, 22
Multiples of 7: 7, 14, 21   LCM: 14
3. Multiples of 3: 3, 6, 9, 12, 15, 18, 21, 24, 27
Multiples of 8: 8, 16, 24, 32   LCM: 24
4. Multiples of 5: 5, 10, 15, 20, 25, 30, 35, 40, 45, 50
Multiples of 9: 9, 18, 27, 36, 45, 54   LCM: 45

Activity 9 (page 7)
1. 8   **2.** 6   **3.** 12   **4.** 9   **5.** 15   **6.** 40
7. 10   **8.** 35   **9.** 6   **10.** 8   **11.** 12   **12.** 8

Activity 10 (page 7)
1. $1\frac{1}{5}$ **2.** $2\frac{1}{4}$ **3.** 2   **4.** $3\frac{3}{5}$ **5.** 9   **6.** $6\frac{2}{3}$
7. $5\frac{2}{3}$ **8.** $5\frac{4}{5}$ **9.** $6\frac{2}{7}$ **10.** $8\frac{1}{4}$ **11.** $7\frac{1}{7}$ **12.** $8\frac{1}{2}$

Activity 11 (page 8)
1. $\frac{8}{2}$ **2.** $\frac{12}{2}$ **3.** $\frac{20}{2}$ **4.** $\frac{30}{5}$ **5.** $\frac{32}{4}$
6. $\frac{27}{9}$ **7.** $\frac{21}{3}$ **8.** $\frac{24}{6}$ **9.** $\frac{20}{10}$

Activity 12 (page 8)
1. $\frac{3}{2}$ **2.** $\frac{7}{3}$ **3.** $\frac{13}{4}$ **4.** $\frac{17}{5}$ **5.** $\frac{30}{7}$
6. $\frac{21}{8}$ **7.** $\frac{24}{7}$ **8.** $\frac{20}{3}$ **9.** $\frac{22}{4}$

Activity 13 (page 9)
1. $\frac{1}{2}$ **2.** $\frac{6}{7}$ **3.** $\frac{1}{2}$ **4.** $\frac{1}{5}$ **5.** $\frac{1}{8}$
6. $\frac{2}{7}$ **7.** $\frac{1}{3}$ **8.** $\frac{1}{9}$ **9.** $\frac{2}{5}$

Activity 14 (page 9)
1. $\frac{5}{8}$ **2.** 1   **3.** $\frac{3}{5}$ **4.** $\frac{2}{3}$ **5.** $1\frac{1}{12}$
6. $\frac{7}{11}$ **7.** $\frac{4}{5}$ **8.** 1   **9.** $1\frac{5}{18}$

Activity 15 (page 10)
1. $\frac{5}{6}$ **2.** $\frac{5}{8}$ **3.** $\frac{11}{15}$ **4.** $1\frac{7}{40}$ **5.** $\frac{11}{15}$
6. $\frac{3}{16}$ **7.** $\frac{8}{9}$ **8.** $\frac{3}{4}$ **9.** $1\frac{13}{28}$

Activity 16 (page 10)
1. $\frac{1}{2}$ **2.** $\frac{1}{2}$ **3.** $\frac{2}{5}$ **4.** $\frac{2}{3}$ **5.** $\frac{5}{8}$
6. $\frac{1}{12}$ **7.** $\frac{1}{4}$ **8.** $\frac{11}{25}$ **9.** $\frac{1}{4}$

Activity 17 (page 11)
1. $\frac{2}{5}$ 2. $1\frac{1}{10}$ 3. $\frac{1}{16}$ 4. $\frac{3}{4}$ 5. $\frac{5}{12}$
6. $\frac{1}{6}$ 7. $\frac{1}{2}$ 8. $\frac{1}{6}$ 9. $\frac{1}{9}$

Activity 18 (page 11)
1. $\frac{11}{12}$ cup   2. $\frac{4}{15}$

Activity 19 (page 12)
1. $\frac{3}{8}$ 2. $\frac{1}{4}$ 3. 1   4. $\frac{1}{2}$ 5. $\frac{1}{4}$
6. $\frac{1}{20}$ 7. $\frac{5}{8}$ 8. $\frac{1}{5}$ 9. $\frac{9}{64}$

Activity 20 (page 12)
1. $1\frac{2}{3}$ 2. $1\frac{1}{8}$ 3. $\frac{4}{5}$ 4. $\frac{7}{12}$ 5. 1
6. $1\frac{1}{5}$ 7. $\frac{9}{16}$ 8. $\frac{2}{3}$ 9. $\frac{5}{14}$

Activity 21 (page 13)
1. 4   2. 9   3. 9   4. 25   5. 27
6. 4   7. 19   8. 12   9. 28

Activity 22 (page 13)
1. $\frac{1}{4}$ 2. 1   3. $\frac{3}{8}$ 4. 9   5. 1   6. $2\frac{1}{4}$

Activity 23 (page 14)
1. c   2. a   3. a   4. b   5. b

Activity 24 (page 14)
1. a   2. c   3. a   4. b   5. b

Activity 25 (page 15)
1. 43   2. 131   3. 28   4. 35. 2
5. 230.0   6. 108.9   7. 609.91   8. 3.43
9. 26.31   10. 1.568   11. 74.132   12. 3,256.099

Activity 26 (page 15)
1. 0.75   2. 0.33   3. 0.40   4. 0.60
5. 0.50   6. 0.78   7. 0.67   8. 0.08
9. 0.60

Activity 27 (page 16)
1. 13,467.99   2. 330.0085   3. 133,698.7
4. 4,500   5. 2,819.19   6. 256.9
7. 0.27007   8. 21.34599   9. 2.0007813
10. 0.29775   11. 45.6123   12. 0.0000007

Activity 28 (page 16)
1. 4   2. -3   3. $4.56 \cdot 10^8$ 4. $9.46 \cdot 10^{-7}$
5. $9.3 \cdot 10^7$ 6. $2.9 \cdot 10^{-3}$

Activity 29 (page 17)
1. 10.2   2. 22.41   3. 23.7   4. 27.08
5. 31.976   6. 1,300.47   7. 2.45   8. 1.94
9. 57.15   10. 332.968   11. 1.978   12. 420.005

Activity 30 (page 17)
1. 206.448   2. 2,390.22   3. 4.176
4. 560.32   5. 1,123.62   6. 1.984
7. 17.1108   8. 1,130.4   9. 11.4767

Activity 31 (page 18)
1. 1.25   2. 17.12   3. 140.616
4. 0.3447   5. 9.031   6. 207.86

Activity 32 (page 18)
1. 153   2. 18.5   3. 3.255
4. 8.3   5. 78   6. 38

Activity 33 (page 19)
1. b   2. a   3. c   4. a   5. c   6. b

Activity 34 (page 19)
1. b   2. a   3. c   4. c   5. b   6. a

Activity 35 (page 20)
1. yes   2. yes   3. no   4. no
5. no   6. yes   7. -14   8. 3
9. 27   10. -578   11. -32   12. 75
13. 42   14. 578   15. 18   16. +3
17. -12   18. -7   19. +8

Activity 36 (page 20)
1. <   2. <   3. =   4. >   5. >   6. >
7. =   8. <   9. <   10. <   11. <   12. <

Activity 37 (page 21)
1. -8, -3, -2, 0, 13, 26   2. -11, -4, -1, 2, 6, 7
3. -7, -5, 0, 5, 33, 38   4. -17, -12, -4, 4, 12, 17
5. -20, -9, 0, 6, 11, 16   6. -6, -2, -1, 3, 4, 5

Activity 38 (page 21)
1. 3   2. -6   3. 34   4. 30   5. 0   6. -17
7. -30   8. 50   9. 34   10. 25   11. -30   12. -30
13. 2   14. 49   15. 297   Bonus: 1

Activity 39 (page 22)
1. 3   2. -2   3. 16   4. -12   5. 16   6. 12
7. -10   8. 26   9. 0   10. 29   11. 40   12. -30
13. 51   14. -20   15. 22   Bonus: 36

Activity 40 (page 22)
1. 24   2. -44   3. 40   4. -42   5. 64   6. 0
7. 150   8. -21   9. 14   10. -72   11. 48   12. -54
13. -100   14. 32   15. -72   Bonus: 60

Activity 41 (page 23)
1. 6   **2.** -7   **3.** -3   **4.** -8   **5.** 2   **6.** -3
7. 4   **8.** 4   **9.** -4   **10.** 3   **11.** 4   **12.** 8
13. 6   **14.** -12   **15.** 6   Bonus: -3

Activity 42 (page 23)
1. 3   **2.** 8   **3.** 0   **4.** 10   **5.** 17   **6.** 21
7. -19   **8.** 40   **9.** -20   **10.** 18   **11.** 8   **12.** 13
Bonus: 26

Activity 43 (page 24)
1. $n + 7$ **2.** $n - 8$ **3.** $2n$ **4.** $n + 12$ **5.** $5n$
6. $n - (-8)$ **7.** $n + 2n$ **8.** $|n| + 3$ **9.** $4n + (n - 1)$

Activity 44 (page 24)
1. 10   **2.** 7   **3.** 6   **4.** 8   **5.** 4   **6.** 12
7. 4   **8.** 2   **9.** 31   **10.** 9   **11.** 7   **12.** 7

Activity 45 (page 25)
1. 6^3 **2.** 4^4 **3.** 5^2 **4.** x^5
5. $(-7)^3$ **6.** $(-b)^2$ **7.** $11 \cdot 11$ **8.** $7 \cdot 7 \cdot 7$
9. $(-4)(-4)(-4)(-4)$ **10.** 8   **11.** 625   **12.** 81

Activity 46 (page 25)
1. 7^8 **2.** 9^4 **3.** r^9 **4.** m^5 **5.** 2,187
6. 7,776   **7.** 512   **8.** 343

Activity 47 (page 26)
1. $\dfrac{1}{8^2}$ **2.** $\dfrac{1}{n^{15}}$ **3.** $\dfrac{1}{5^5}$ **4.** $\dfrac{x}{y^3}$

5. 4^{-6} **6.** 11^{-2} **7.** xy^{-5} **8.** mn^{-4}

Activity 48 (page 26)
1. 15   **2.** 6   **3.** 40   **4.** 80
5. 9   **6.** -1   **7.** 23   **8.** 12

Activity 49 (page 27)
1. $\$7h$ **2.** $\$0.50c$ **3.** $b + 2$ **4.** $200 - s$

Activity 50 (page 27)
1. b   **2.** d   **3.** c   **4.** a

Activity 51 (page 28)
1. $7 + c = 15$ **2.** $d \cdot 3 = 12$ **3.** $m + 8 = 10$
4. $6 \cdot k = 30$ **5.** $11 + x = 21$ **6.** $4 \cdot r = 16$
7. $x + z + y = 28$ **or** $z + x + y = 28$ **8.** $s \cdot 7 = 42$
9. $5 + 9 + 2 = 16$ **or** $9 + 5 + 2 = 16$ **10.** $q \cdot p = 72$

Activity 52 (page 28)
1. $(45 + 55) + 38 = 138$ **2.** $43 + (92 + 8) = 143$
3. $(6 + 4) + 37 = 47$ **4.** $36 + (12 + 8) = 56$
5. $(31 + 9) + (15 + 5) = 60$ **6.** $(4 \cdot 5) \cdot 7 = 140$

7. $48 \cdot (2 \cdot 5) = 480$ **8.** $(20 \cdot 5) \cdot 39 = 3,900$
9. $(10 \cdot 10)(15 \cdot 10) = 15,000$
10. $(-2 \cdot 5) \cdot 96 = -960$

Activity 53 (page 29)
1. $(5 \cdot 4) + (5 \cdot 5)$ **2.** $4w + 9w$ **3.** $6m + 6n$
4. $12b + 9c$ **5.** $9v + 6$ **6.** $10h + 12$
7. $17g + 18$ **8.** $19s + 20$

Activity 54 (page 29)
1. 47   **2.** 72   **3.** 65   **4.** 0
5. 46   **6.** 69   **7.** 0   **8.** 32

Activity 55 (page 30)
1. $5x + 3y$ **2.** $t + 2s$ **3.** $5m - 2n$
4. $5a - 4b$ **5.** $10c - 4d$ **6.** $-f + 2g$
7. $4j - 5h$ **8.** $10w + 7v$ **9.** $2y + 6z$
10. $6a + 5b + c$ **11.** $2h + i + 3j$ **12.** $3n + p$

Activity 56 (page 30)
1. $4x + 12$ **2.** $8m - 48$ **3.** $6b - 3$
4. $-16n$ **5.** $x + 8$ **6.** $8c - 6$
7. $12m - 26$ **8.** $9g + 9h$ **9.** $2d + c + 7$
10. $-5x + 2y - 2$ **11.** $3b - 10$ **12.** $4a + 4b$

Activity 57 (page 31)
1. $y = 3$ **2.** $m = 5$ **3.** $b = 5$ **4.** $z = 4$
5. $n = 14$ **6.** $x = 0$ **7.** $m = -4$ **8.** $z = -8$
9. $w = 0$ **10.** $n = -6$

Activity 58 (page 31)
1. $b = 6$ **2.** $m = 11$ **3.** $n = 11$ **4.** $y = 10$
5. $a = 9$ **6.** $v = 4$ **7.** $t = 7$ **8.** $c = 5$
9. $m = 37$ **10.** $b = 1$

Activity 59 (page 32)
1. $m = 5$ **2.** $b = 15$ **3.** $n = -4$ **4.** $v = 3$
5. $s = 16$ **6.** $g = 6$ **7.** $y = 9$ **8.** $k = 8$
9. $z = 3$ **10.** $h = 27$

Activity 60 (page 32)
1. $28 + w = 42$; $\$14$ **2.** $c - 24 = 30$; 54
3. $a - \$15.98 = \$4.02$; $20   **4.** $58 + b = 80$; 22

Activity 61 (page 33)
1. $m = 8$ **2.** $t = 4$ **3.** $a = 9$ **4.** $x = 11$
5. $p = 3$ **6.** $z = 10$ **7.** $y = -7$ **8.** $g = 6$
9. $t = \frac{1}{3}$ **10.** $j = \frac{1}{4}$

Activity 62 (page 33)
1. $x = 20$ **2.** $m = 16$ **3.** $g = 50$ **4.** $n = 0$
5. $w = 12$ **6.** $k = -12$ **7.** $h = 45$ **8.** $c = 99$
9. $v = 54$ **10.** $t = 49$

Activity 63 (page 34)
1. $a = -15$ 2. $b = 6$ 3. $n = 6$ 4. $w = 35$
5. $y = 36$ 6. $x = 12$ 7. $u = -5$ 8. $r = 48$
9. $d = 16$ 10. $g = 9$

Activity 64 (page 34)
1. $12c = 84; 7$ 2. $9b = \$4.05; \$0.45$
3. $6w = \$54; \$9$ 4. $\frac{m}{8} = \$1.95; \$15.60$

Activity 65 (page 35)
1. $x = 2$ 2. $y = 3$ 3. $m = 3$ 4. $d = 4$
5. $h = -8$ 6. $n = 6$ 7. $b = 3$ 8. $f = 8$
9. $a = 4$ 10. $p = 3$

Activity 66 (page 35)
1. $t = 44$ 2. $b = 15$ 3. $x = 8$ 4. $m = 21$
5. $z = 20$ 6. $w = 9$ 7. $y = 90$ 8. $r = 18$
9. $u = 20$ 10. $p = 32$

Activity 67 (page 36)
1. $8n + 12 = 60; 6$ 2. $7n + 3 = 38; 5$
3. $5n + 10 = 55; 9$ 4. $\frac{n}{4} + 7 = 15; 32$
5. $9n - 5 = 31; 4$

Activity 68 (page 36)
1. b   2. a   3. b   4. c

Activity 69 (page 37)
1. $x = 5$ 2. $n = 4$ 3. $b = 3$ 4. $t = -2$
5. $s = 6$ 6. $y = 8$ 7. $t = 2$ 8. $r = 7$
9. $m = 33$ 10. $p = -5$

Activity 70 (page 37)
1. $n = 9$ 2. $z = 4$ 3. $t = 5$ 4. $k = 3$
5. $r = 7$ 6. $c = 21$ 7. $h = 2$ 8. $t = -5$
9. $g = 6$ 10. $j = 4$

Activity 71 (page 38)
1. 420 miles   2. 22 cm   3. 40 in.^{2}
4. 990 miles   5. 42 in.   6. 27 cm^2

Activity 72 (page 38)
1. 6 hours   2. 60 mph   3. 3   4. 5

Activity 73 (page 39)
1. yes   2. no   3. no   4. yes
5. no   6. $x \geq 46$ 7. $p \leq 200$ 8. $r \geq 52$
9. $b \geq 6$ 10. $c < 12$

Activity 74 (page 39)
Any variables are acceptable.
1. $y < 4$ 2. $x \geq -3$ 3. $n \leq 0$ 4. $t > -1$
5. $m \geq 2$ 6. $b < 6$ 7. $z \leq 5$ 8. $h \geq -4$

Activity 75 (page 40)
1.
2.
3.
4.
5.
6.
7.
8.

Activity 76 (page 40)
1. $x < 2$
2. $y > 5$
3. $a \leq -4$
4. $r < 6$
5. $s \geq -2$
6. $t > 0$

Activity 77 (page 41)
1. $q \geq 4$
2. $n < 3$
3. $c > -1$
4. $x \leq 2$
5. $s < 6$
6. $y \geq -4$

Activity 78 (page 41)
1. b   2. a   3. a   4. c   5. c   6. b

Activity 79 (page 42)
1. K   2. C   3. M   4. A   5. F   6. L
7. (2, 3)   8. (6, -5)   9. (-5, -4)   10. (0, -4)
11. (-6, -3)   12. (-1, -1)   13. (5, 1)   14. (-5, 6)

Activity 80 (page 42)

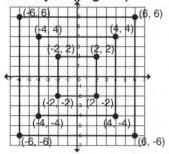

Activity 81 (page 43)

1. yes   **2.** no   **3.** no   **4.** no
5. no   **6.** yes   **7.** 10   **8.** 6
9. 2   **10.** -14   **11.** -10   **12.** -6

Activity 82 (page 43)

1.

x	y
0	-4
-1	-7
2	2
3	5

2.

x	y
4	2
1	5
0	6
6	0

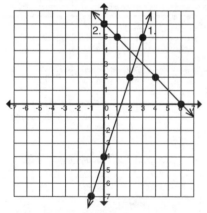

Activity 83 (page 44)

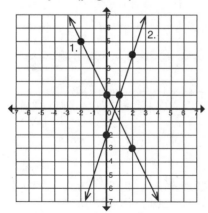

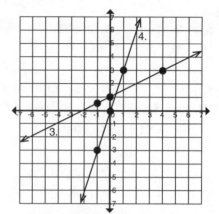

Activity 84 (page 44)

1. 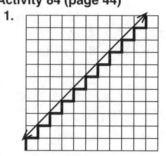   **2.**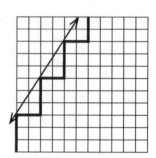

3. 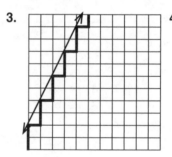   **4.**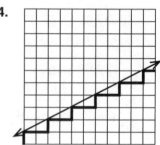

Activity 85 (page 45)

1. $\frac{3}{4}$ **2.** 2   **3.** $\frac{1}{2}$ **4.** 1

Activity 86 (page 45)

1. -3   **2.** $-\frac{1}{2}$ **3.** -2   **4.** 0

Activity 87 (page 46)

1. $-\frac{1}{3}$ **2.** -3   **3.** $\frac{1}{2}$ **4.** $\frac{1}{3}$ **5.** 1   **6.** 1

Activity 88 (page 46)

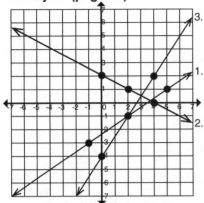

Activity 89 (page 47)

1. x-intercept: -1; y-intercept: 2
2. x-intercept: 1; y-intercept: 1
3. x-intercept: 1; y-intercept: -3

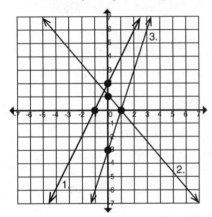

Activity 90 (page 47)

1. slope: $\frac{1}{3}$ y-intercept: -6
2. slope: -3   y-intercept: 4
3. slope: $-\frac{2}{5}$ y-intercept: $-\frac{1}{2}$
4. slope: 4   y-intercept: -2

Activity 91 (page 48)

1. y-intercept: -4; slope: $\frac{1}{3}$; equation: $y = \frac{1}{3}x - 4$
2. y-intercept: 2; slope: $\frac{2}{3}$; equation: $y = \frac{2}{3}x + 2$

Activity 92 (page 48)

1. $y = -\frac{2}{3}x + 3$ 2. $y = -3x + 6$
3. $y = \frac{1}{2}x + 2$ 4. $y = \frac{5}{4}x - 3$

Activity 93 (page 49)

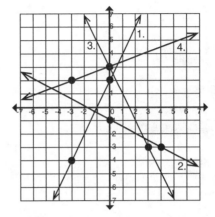

Activity 94 (page 49)

1. b   2. a   3. d   4. b

Activity 95 (page 50)

1.

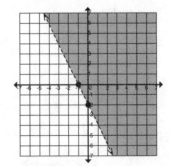

2.

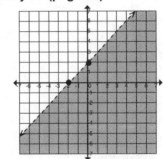

3.

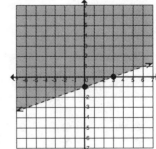

89

4.

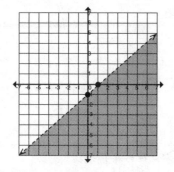

Activity 96 (page 50)
   1. (-2, 2)   **2.** (0, 0)   **3.** (2, -2)

Activity 97 (page 51)
   1. (-1, 2)   **2.** (1, -1)   **3.** (0, 3)

Activity 98 (page 51)
Parallel lines

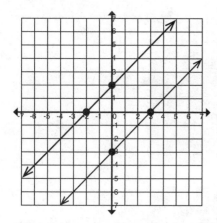

Activity 99 (page 52)
   1. $\frac{4}{1}$ = 4   **2.** $\frac{1}{2}$ **3.** $\frac{1}{3}$ **4.** $\frac{1}{4}$ **5.** $\frac{2}{5}$
   6. $\frac{5}{11}$ **7.** $\frac{3}{2}$ **8.** $\frac{2}{9}$ **9.** $\frac{8}{13}$ **10.** $\frac{1}{50}$

Activity 100 (page 52)
   1. $4/ticket   **2.** $3/gallon   **3.** 0.3 inches/hr.
   4. $0.85/lb.   **5.** 62.5 mph   **6.** $0.54/oz.

Activity 101 (page 53)
Answers will vary—some possibilities listed here:
   1. $\frac{6}{8}, \frac{12}{16}$ **2.** $\frac{2}{12}, \frac{3}{18}$ **3.** $\frac{20}{24}, \frac{50}{60}$
   4. $\frac{8}{18}, \frac{12}{27}$ **5.** $\frac{18}{20}, \frac{27}{30}$ **6.** $\frac{4}{10}, \frac{6}{15}$

Activity 102 (page 53)
   1. yes   **2.** yes   **3.** no   **4.** 2   **5.** 12
   6. 30   **7.** 6.25   **8.** 14   **9.** 42

Activity 103 (page 54)
   1. $\frac{4}{100} = \frac{x}{20}$; $5
   2. $\frac{4}{100} = \frac{12}{g}$; 300 miles
   3. $\frac{42}{3} = \frac{x}{8}$; $112
   4. $\frac{3}{5} = \frac{p}{30}$; 18 pages

Activity 104 (page 54)
   1. $\frac{3}{20}$ **2.** $\frac{1}{5}$ **3.** $\frac{8}{25}$ **4.** $1\frac{1}{4}$ **5.** 1
   6. $\frac{1}{2}$ **7.** $\frac{33}{50}$ **8.** $\frac{7}{10}$ **9.** $\frac{3}{5}$

Activity 105 (page 55)
   1. 0.74   **2.** 0.06   **3.** 1.5   **4.** 4
   5. 2.5   **6.** 0.037   **7.** 0.05   **8.** 0.75
   9. 0.1   **10.** 0.0225   **11.** 2.58   **12.** 0.065

Activity 106 (page 55)
   1. 50%   **2.** 67%   **3.** 59%   **4.** 3%   **5.** 70%
   6. 250%   **7.** 600%   **8.** 9%   **9.** 80%

Activity 107 (page 56)
   1. 50%   **2.** 40%   **3.** 25%   **4.** 80%   **5.** 250%
   6. 200%   **7.** 75%   **8.** 60%   **9.** 150%

Activity 108 (page 56)
   1. $\frac{3}{4}$; 75%   **2.** 60%   **3.** 40%   **4.** 50%

Activity 109 (page 57)
   1. 90   **2.** 15   **3.** 22   **4.** 3.4
   5. 40   **6.** 147   **7.** 0.48   **8.** 4.5

Activity 110 (page 57)
   1. 50%   **2.** 33.$\overline{3}$%   **3.** 20%   **4.** 10%
   5. 5%   **6.** 25%   **7.** 20%   **8.** 25%

Activity 111 (page 58)
   1. 80   **2.** 150   **3.** 75   **4.** 64
   5. 70   **6.** 200   **7.** 500   **8.** 50

Activity 112 (page 58)
   1. 51   **2.** 15%   **3.** $300   **4.** $375

Activity 113 (page 59)
   1. 50% increase   **2.** 75% decrease
   3. 66.7% increase   **4.** 100% increase
   5. 60% decrease   **6.** 100% decrease
   7. 19% decrease   **8.** 25% increase

Activity 114 (page 59)
1. b   2. c   3. b   4. a   5. a   6. c

Activity 115 (page 60)
1. >   2. =   3. <   4. <   5. <   6. >
7. >   8. >   9. =

Activity 116 (page 60)
1. $-\frac{5}{24}$ 2. $-\frac{3}{10}$ 3. $1\frac{1}{16}$ 4. $-1\frac{1}{8}$
5. $-\frac{7}{18}$ 6. $-\frac{5}{6}$ 7. 1.9   8. 10.3
9. -21.5   10. 1.77   11. 16.15   12. -18.7

Activity 117 (page 61)
1. $-\frac{3}{20}$ 2. $\frac{11}{12}$ 3. $-2\frac{1}{2}$ 4. $\frac{3}{10}$
5. $\frac{7}{24}$ 6. $\frac{1}{8}$ 7. -10.3   8. 21.8
9. 188.5   10. -6.26   11. -1.52   12. 1.8

Activity 118 (page 61)
1. 1   2. $-\frac{1}{6}$ 3. $-\frac{5}{8}$ 4. $1\frac{1}{2}$
5. $3\frac{1}{16}$ 6. $10\frac{2}{3}$ 7. 3.84   8. -8.37
9. 23.925   10. -39   11. 17.262   12. -33

Activity 119 (page 62)
1. $1\frac{1}{2}$ 2. $-\frac{3}{8}$ 3. -3   4. $1\frac{1}{2}$
5. $-1\frac{1}{3}$ 6. $\frac{15}{16}$ 7. 9.2   8. -2.2
9. $6.3\overline{6}$ 10. 1.5   11. 0.65   12. -400

Activity 120 (page 62)
1. $1\frac{2}{3}$ 2. $\frac{8}{15}$ 3. 3   4. -5
5. $-\frac{4}{7}$ 6. -2   7. -3   8. $-1\frac{5}{7}$

Activity 121 (page 63)
1. 6   2. 13.5   3. -3   4. -28
5. 12.4   6. 4.5   7. 14.5   8. -1

Activity 122 (page 63)
1. -4   2. 2   3. 0   4. $\frac{1}{11}$
5. 3   6. $\frac{5}{9}$ 7. -6   8. 1

Activity 123 (page 64)
1. $x = \pm 4$ 2. $b = \pm 5$ 3. $r = \pm 6$ 4. $d = \pm 10$
5. $n = \pm 12$ 6. $h = \pm 8$ 7. $c = \pm 9$ 8. $t = \pm 20$

Activity 124 (page 64)
1. 7   2. 11   3. 1   4. 13
5. -2   6. -15   7. -10   8. -14

Activity 125 (page 65)
1. 2   2. 7   3. 9   4. 5
5. 15   6. 12   7. 16   8. 2

Activity 126 (page 65)
1. 25   2. 9   3. 70   4. 8
5. 6   6. 42   7. 16   8. -55

Activity 127 (page 66)
1. 9   2. 4   3. 10   4. 7
5. -7   6. -3   7. -10   8. -1

Activity 128 (page 66)
1. $\frac{3}{4}$ 2. 2   3. $-\frac{1}{3}$ 4. $\frac{7}{9}$
5. $1\frac{1}{11}$ 6. $-\frac{1}{2}$ 7. $-\frac{13}{15}$ 8. $\frac{1}{2}$

Activity 129 (page 67)
1. b   2. a   3. a   4. c   5. c   6. a

Activity 130 (page 67)
1. c   2. a   3. b   4. a   5. b   6. a

Activity 131 (page 68)
1. 6   2. 7   3. 4   4. 8
5. 9   6. 10   7. 5   8. 3

Activity 132 (page 68)
1. 5   2. 17   3. 12   4. 8   5. 16   6. 25

Activity 133 (page 69)
1. 15.6 ft.   2. 20 inches   3. 8.5 inches   4. 12 ft.

Activity 134 (page 69)
1. 50.24 cm^2 2. 200.96 cm^2 3. 10 cm   4. 40 cm

Activity 135 (page 70)
1. binomial   2. mononomial   3. trinomial
4. trinomial   5. mononomial   6. binomial
7. trinomial   8. mononomial   9. binomial
10. trinomial

Activity 136 (page 70)
1. 3   2. 2   3. 6   4. 5
5. 4   6. -4   7. -1   8. 7

Activity 137 (page 71)
1. 2, 4   2. -3, -6   3. 10, 1
4. $5x + 11y$ 5. $6n + m$ 6. $2r^2 + 4r + 1$
7. $3g^3 + 2g^2 + 5g$ 8. $3c^2d - cd$
9. $-3w^4 + 2w^3 + 2v^3$

Activity 138 (page 71)
1. $-3c + 11$ 2. $11r + 5s + 9t$ 3. $6x + 13$
4. $11a^2 + 3b$ 5. $7x^2 - x$ 6. $5r + 3s$
7. $5x^2 + 7x$ 8. $3a^2 + 3b^2$

Activity 139 (page 72)
1. $8x + 20$ 2. $12n + 6$ 3. $14c + 14$

Activity 140 (page 72)
1. $2g^2 + 3g$ 2. $2x + y$ 3. $b^2 + 2b$ 4. $-w$
5. $r^2 + s$ 6. $3e + 7f$ 7. $3d^2 + 3e$ 8. $4m^2 - 2n$

Activity 141 (page 73)
1. a^7 2. $12t$ 3. $6x^2$ 4. $-12b$
5. $-6m^2n$ 6. $-24g^6$ 7. $-27s^3$ 8. $-6k^7$

Activity 142 (page 73)
1. 2^4 2. $16x^6$ 3. $-125b^3c^3$ 4. r^{-6}
5. f^6g^{12} 6. y^6z^2 7. j^{15} 8. $a^6b^6c^6$

Activity 143 (page 74)
1. $5n + 20$ 2. $3a^2 + 15a$ 3. $5t^2 + 15t$
4. $3b^2 + 6b$ 5. $6mn + 2mp$ 6. $18x^2 + 6xy$
7. $6r^2 + 9rs + 12rt$ 8. $5k^2 - 10kj - 35kp$

Activity 144 (page 74)
1. 12   2. 15   3. 15   4. 10
5. 20   6. 10   7. -12   8. 84

Activity 145 (page 75)
1. $3n^2 + 1$ 2. $4b + 1$ 3. $3t + 1$
4. $m + 1$ 5. $4a + 2$ 6. $y^2 + y$

Activity 146 (page 75)
1. $n^2 + 9n + 20$ 2. $6b^2 - 26b + 24$
3. $4t^2 - 19t - 5$ 4. $x^2 - 18x + 81$
5. $2g^2 - 8$ 6. $6a^2 - 7a - 20$

Activity 147 (page 76)
1. $4x^2$ 2. $3y^2 + 12y$ 3. $5z^2 + 25z$

Activity 148 (page 76)
1. Jasper   2. Southbend
3. Sunville   4. 159 miles

Activity 149 (page 77)
1. c, $20   2. a, $26   3. b, $16.50

Activity 150 (page 77)
1. $10d + 5(12 - d) = 90$; 6 dimes, 6 nickels
2. $25q + 5(7 - q) = 75$: 2 quarters, 5 nickels
3. $25q + 10(6 - q) = 90$; 2 quarters, 4 dimes
4. $10d + 5(9 - d) = 70$; 5 dimes, 4 nickels

Activity 151 (page 78)
1. b   2. a   3. a   4. c   5. b   6. c

Activity 152 (page 78)
1. a   2. c   3. a   4. b   5. b   6. c

Activity 153 (page 79)
1. Rule: subtract 2; next 3 terms: 2, 0, -2
2. Rule: add 25; next 3 terms: 225, 250, 275
3. Rule: add 0.3; next 3 terms: 4.5, 4.8, 5.1
4. Rule: multiply by 3; next 3 terms: 324; 972; 2,916
5. Rule: divide by 10; next 3 terms: 0.094, 0.0094, 0.00094
6. Rule: multiply by $\frac{1}{2}$; next 3 terms: $\frac{1}{32}, \frac{1}{64}, \frac{1}{128}$

Activity 154 (page 79)
1. B; 63   2. D; 365   3. E; 65,536
4. C; 3,263,442   5. A; 756,030

Activity 155 (page 80)
1. 6   2. 12   3. 72   4. 36

Activity 156 (page 80)
1. 5,040   2. 3,628,800   3. 90   4. 665,280
5. 362,760   6. 4   7. 5   8. 42

Activity 157 (page 81)
1. $\frac{1}{6}$ 2. $\frac{3}{6} = \frac{1}{2}$ 3. $\frac{4}{6} = \frac{2}{3}$ 4. $\frac{3}{6} = \frac{1}{2}$
5. $\frac{2}{6} = \frac{1}{3}$ 6. 0   7. $\frac{5}{6}$ 8. $\frac{5}{6}$

Activity 158 (page 81)
1. D   2. D   3. I   4. I   5. I   6. D

Activity 159 (page 82)
1. $\frac{1}{36}$ 2. $\frac{1}{4}$ 3. $\frac{1}{4}$ 4. $\frac{1}{12}$ 5. $\frac{1}{12}$ 6. $\frac{5}{9}$

Activity 160 (page 82)
1. 4 to 11   2. 17 to 13   3. 2 to 1
4. 13 to 17   5. 23 to 7   6. 3 to 2

Activity 161 (page 83)
1. 300   2. 150   3. 73   4. 160

Activity 162 (page 83)
1. 2%   2. 1.5%   3. yes   4. 120